Dhyan Manik

Sounds of the Thai Language

Book I

– Basic Sounds

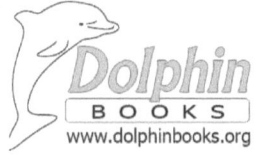
www.dolphinbooks.org

22 Secrets of Learning Thai

Copyright © Dhyan Manik and Dolphin Books 2020
Cover design, layout and phonetic pictures: Uri Hautamäki, Data Graphics
Thai consonant pictures: Studio Aun

Audio spoken in MP3 format by native speakers can be downloaded from the following address: www.thaibooks.net

Thai voices: Ms. Waree Singhanart
                 Mr. Watit Pumyoo
English voice: Mr. Mark Harris

Publisher:
Dolphin Books
info@dolphinbooks.org
www.dolphinbooks.org

ISBN 978-9526651323

Table of Contents

Book I – Basic Sounds
Secrets 1-15 ISBN 978-9526651323

Introduction 12
   Introduction 12
   How to use this book 12
   A history of the Thai language 13
   Characteristics of the Thai language 14
   Pronunciation 15
   Transliteration 16
   Sounds 17
   Tones 18
   The Thai writing system 20
   Learning Thai: main obstacles 21

I. Introduction to basic phonetics

Secret 1 24
   Introduction to basic phonetics 24
   Important consonant qualities 25
   Important vowel qualities 29
   Place of articulation 31
   Sound exercise 1 32
   Practical learning tips 34
   Reading exercise 1 34

II. Basic sounds

Secret 2 36
   Stop lip sounds p ป, b บ 36
   Closed vowel sounds i อิ, ii อี 40
   Sound exercise 2 42
   Practical learning tips 43
   Reading exercise 2 43

Secret 3 45
   Stop lip sounds ph พ, ph ผ 45
   Closed vowel sounds ù อึ, uu อื 47
   Sound exercise 3 50
   Practical learning tips 51
   Reading exercise 3 51

Secret 4 53
   Fricative lip-teeth sounds f ฟ, f ฝ 53
   Closed vowel sounds ù อุ, uu อู 56
   Sound exercise 4 58
   Practical learning tips 59
   Reading exercise 4 59

Secret 5 61
   Stop teeth sounds th ท, th ถ 61
   Half open vowel sounds è เอะ, ee เอ 64
   Sound exercise 5 66
   Practical learning tips 67
   Reading exercise 5 67

Secret 6 69
   Stop teeth sounds t ต, d ด 69
   Half open vowel sounds è เออะ, ออ ออ 74
   Sound exercise 6 75
   Practical learning tips 76
   Reading exercise 6 77

Secret 7 80
    Fricative teeth sounds s ซ, s ส 80
    Half open vowel sounds ò โอะ, oo โอ 83
    Sound exercise 7 85
    Practical learning tips 86
    Reading exercise 7 86

Secret 8 89
    Stop front sounds tʃ ช, tʃ ฉ, ts จ 89
    Open vowel sounds ɛ̀ แอะ, ɛɛ แอ 95
    Sound exercise 8 97
    Practical learning tips 98
    Reading exercise 8 99

Secret 9 101
    Stop back sounds kh ข, kh ค, k ก 101
    Open vowel sounds à อะ, aa อา 106
    Sound exercise 9 108
    Practical learning tips 109
    Reading exercise 9 109

Secret 10 114
    Fricative glottal sounds h ฮ and h ห 114
    Open vowel sounds ò เอาะ, ɔɔ ออ 116
    Sound exercise 10 118
    Practical learning tips 120
    Reading exercise 10 120

Secret 11 126
    Sonorant consonant sounds m ม, n น 126
    Special vowels am อำ, au เอา 129
    Sound exercise 11 131
    Practical learning tips 133
    Reading exercise 11 134

Secret 12 139
    Sonorant consonant sounds l ล, r ร 139
    Special vowels ai ใอ, ai ไอ 143

Sound exercise 12	144
Practical learning tips	145
Reading exercise 12	146

Secret 13 150
    Sonorant consonant sounds ng ງ 150
    Diphthongs ia ເxຍະ, iia ເxຍ 152
    Sound exercise 13 154
    Practical learning tips 155
    Reading exercise 13 155

Secret 14 160
    Sonorant consonant sound y ຍ 160
    Diphthongs ɯa ເxືອະ, ɯɯa ເxືອ 162
    Sound exercise 14 164
    Practical learning tips 165
    Reading exercise 14 167

Secret 15 172
    Sonorant consonant sound w ວ 172
    Diphthongs ua xົວະ, uua xົວ 174
    Sound exercise 15 175
    Practical learning tips 176
    Reading exercise 15 177

Book II – Advanced Sounds

Secrets 16-22 ISBN 978-9526651330

III. Vowel combinations

Secret 16 12
  Short vowel combinations with two sounds iu ອິວ, ui ອຸຍ, eu ເອິ້ວ, ai ອັຍ 13
  Sound exercise 16a 17
  Practical learning tips 19
  Long vowel combinations with two sounds
  eeu ເອວ, əəi ເອຍ, ooi ໂອຍ, ɛɛu ແອວ, aai ອາຍ, aau ອາວ, ɔɔi ອອຍ 19
  Sound exercise 16b 26
  Practical learning tips 29
  Long vowel combinations with three sounds
  iiau ເອຍວ, ɯɯai ເອືອຍ, uuai ອວຍ 29
  Sound exercise 16c 33
  Practical learning tips 35
  Reading exercise 16 36

IV. Consonant clusters

Secret 17 42
  Consonant clusters 42
  Sound exercise 17 43
  Practical learning tips 46
  Reading exercise 17 48

V. Comparing sounds

Secret 18 54
  Same sound but different tone 54
  Sound exercise 18a 55
  Similar consonant sounds 56
  Sound exercise 18b 57
  Consonant sounds that do not exist in English 58
  Sound exercise 18c 60

Similar vowel sounds 61
Sound exercise 18d 61
Vowel sounds that do not exist in Standard English 63
Sound exercise 18e 64
Practical learning tips 66
Reading exercise 18 66

VI. Final sounds

Secret 19 72
Final sounds – closed ending 72
Sound exercise 19a 74
Final sounds – Open ending 76
Sound exercise 19b 77
Practical learning tips 79
Reading exercise 19 80

VII. Tones of the Thai language

Secret 20 86
Tones of the Thai language 87
Tone rules without tone marks 91
Tone rule for normal tone 91
Tone rule for low tone 92
Tone rule for falling tone 93
Tone rule for high tone 94
Tone rule for rising tone 95
Tone rules with tone marks 96
Tone rules for special tone regulators อ and ห 99
Special rules for two-syllable words 100
Tones minimized 103
Tone mismatch between writing and speaking 105
Sound exercise 20 106
Practical learning tips 110
Reading exercise 20 111

Secret 21 116
    Complete list of Thai vowels 116
    Vowels and their written forms 117
    Vowels written under the consonant 117
    Vowels written before the consonant 118
    Vowels written around the consonant 119
    Vowel sounds pronounced but not written 123
    Sounds written with the vowel-shortening symbol 124
    The long ee เอ -symbol as a part in other sounds 125
    Vowels with irregular pronunciation 126
    Special rules for the letter ร ฮ 127
    Sound exercise 21 129
    Practical learning tips 130
    Reading exercise 21 131

Secret 22 135
    Complete list of consonants according to the alphabetic order 135
    Most common consonants according to consonant classes 138
    Most common and rear consonants according to consonant classes ...140
    Consonants according to the sounds 143
    Summary for the intial consonant sounds 151
    Summary for the final consonant sounds 153
    Summary for tone rules 154
    Consonant letter Thai or foreign origin? 155
    Sound exercise 22 159
    Practical learning tips 161
    Reading exercise 22 163

Acknowledgment

I would like to thank the following people for giving their time and energy to help me to write this book.

First of all, Mr. Watit Pumyoo, Academic Services Center, Faculty of Arts, Chulalongkorn University, Bangkok.

He has given up much of his valuable time in order to sit down with me and go through the whole book. He has significantly improved the phonetic description of the Thai sounds and advised on choosing the right Thai words as examples making it easier for learners to understand the Thai language. His insight in relation to the Thai writing system and sounds of the Thai language has been indispensable. Without his help the book would have not been completed.

Secondly, I would like to thank Miss Waree Singhanart from the Thai Smile Language School, Bangkok for looking over the book with me. She has helped me a great deal with Thai sentences and proofreading the Thai text. All this has been done by her with a smile and great sense of humour.

Thirdly, I am grateful to Mr. Mark Harris, who read the book and suggested various amendments to improve the clarity and style of the written English. He also helped me to see many of the themes of the book from the perspective of those students completely new to the Thai language.

Lastly, I want to thank everybody who is interested in reading this book and learning Thai.

Introduction

How to use this book

Each secret is divided into four parts: A is about learning sounds, B contains sound examples of Thai words, C gives you practical learning tips for studying Thai, and D is an exercise in learning to read Thai and understanding the tone rules.

You may study each secret completely from A to D or focus on any of the four sections consecutively depending on your preferences. The exercises in part D of each secret are mainly for those who are ready to learn the Thai script and read written Thai. You may prefer to study them after you master all the sounds.

The primary aim of the book is to give you a basic knowledge of Thai sounds and tones so that you will be able to go on with your studies to learn this beautiful language. If you want to learn the Thai writing system, this book explains it in a simple way by giving you practical examples and also basic theory.

Even though the function of the book is not to teach you Thai vocabulary, it contains a vast number of words, which can be used in your daily conversations. It also contains a number of practical tips to assist your learning process.

This book will give you a foundation upon which you can build to successfully acquire the skills to fluently communicate with Thai people. The emphasis here is on giving you the right tools for mastering the basic foundation of knowledge required in speaking, understanding, and even reading Thai. As you will soon understand there are a few essential differences in comparison with learning western languages such as English, Spanish or German.

Moreover, as an English speaker, it will be much easier for you to learn any foreign language after you have fully understood the sounds of the Thai language. By comprehending these secrets, you will save a lot of time and learn much faster. Take some time to organize yourself and study this book. Listen to the audio time and again and study each Thai sound, until you understand how to make it both in theory and practice.

A history of the Thai language

Thai is the national language of Thailand. It is spoken by about eighty percent of the total population, which is now over sixty million.

According to history, the Thai alphabet was created by King Ramakamhaeng of Sukhothai in 1283. The script was taken from Pali, Sanskrit, and other Indic languages. Many foreign words from Mon, Khmer and later from English have also been borrowed and adapted into the Thai language.

Spoken Thai has retained its flexibility. Many foreign words have been modified over time to become better suited to Thai sounds. However, written Thai is conservative and has not changed very much since it was introduced in 1283 by the Great King of Sukhothai.

Spoken Thai can be divided into four major dialects. Central Thai is spoken by people in Bangkok and in Central Thailand. It is this Central Thai dialect that is spoken on TV and also taught in schools in Thailand. It is the language of education. Northern Thai is spoken by people in Chiang Mai and around the northwest of Thailand. Southern Thai is spoken in the south. The Isaan dialect is widely spoken in the North-Eastern part of the country.

Thai people can usually understand each other quite easily, since the majority can understand and speak Central Thai. When Isaan people use their own dialect, outsiders would have some difficulty understanding the conversation, since the dialect has borrowed many words from Lao. Therefore, it could be regarded as a language of its own, with similarities to Lao. In addition to the four major dialects, a few other languages like Cambodian, Chinese and some more localised dialects are spoken in Thailand.

Characteristics of the Thai language

Thai language is vowel-oriented in the sense that vowels and vowel combinations play a very important part in the spoken language. Five different tones are attached to vowel sounds. The tones are mainly determined by consonants or tone marks.

The grammar rules in Thai are very straightforward. For instance, a verb is not needed for a sentence to be complete. "You pretty" suffices for "you are pretty". Each and every word is always in its basic form. For example: verbs are not conjugated, there are no tenses for verbs, there are no plural forms for nouns and no genders or articles like a, an or the. As an illustration of this, in English we would say, "I drove him to the school", but the same in Thai would be, "I drive he school". The context would reveal the tense.

Difficulty arises from the fact that there are a vast number of words and synonyms to be used in different situations. As a foreigner you need to learn to use the right word in the right context. You need to consider whom you are talking to and where. This requires some sensitivity on your part to the cultural differences in Thai society.

Since the grammar is simple, the choice of words and their order within the sentence become very important. Some words go together while others do not. There are words that are sometimes placed at the beginning of a sentence, sometimes at the end.

Thai is written from left to right like any major western language. It uses an alphabet and script unfamiliar to most western learners. There are no full stops, commas or question marks, no spaces between words, or even between sentences.

In spite of this, it is recommended that you start learning the Thai script right from the beginning. Knowing it will assist you in other aspects of your language learning.

Pronunciation

As you study this book, take enough time to understand clearly how each sound is produced in Thai. As westerners, we need to understand how to pronounce Thai words correctly. In addition, we have to use the right tone. Tones are a very important part of the Thai language. Learn the sound first, then add the right tone to it.

When you ask Thai people how to pronounce a certain word, it is often difficult to know which of the two you are mispronouncing: the sound or the tone. Thais do not distinguish between sounds and tones, since they are born into the habit. We westerners, however, need to look at these two separately, since it can be challenging for us, at least in the beginning, even to be able to pronounce the word correctly without putting the right tone into it.

While attempting to speak Thai, you may often run into a situation where the Thai person simply does not understand you or thinks you are speaking English. This may be because you do not pronounce the word exactly right, or that Thais, at least in tourist areas, automatically assume you do not speak Thai. Some Thais like to have the exactly correct pronunciation before they are ready to understand you. Others are able to understand you even if you mispronounce a word a bit.

Also, be aware that much of the meaning of words in Thai is understood from the context. If the word you have chosen to use is somewhat unfamiliar in the relevant situation, Thais will have difficulty understanding you even if you were pronouncing it correctly. Many Thai words are pronounced the same, yet have a different meaning. Therefore, you need to learn to use the right word in the right situation. This is much more relevant in Thai than in some major western languages such as English.

Transliteration

You also need to learn how Thai sounds are written in the Roman letters. This process is called transliteration or Romanization of Thai. Be aware that unfortunately there are not one but many different ways to transliterate. This is something you will just have to get used to. Once you have learned all Thai sounds properly, it is easier to understand different transliteration systems.

As far as vowels are concerned, some transliterations are quite difficult to understand. This is due to the fact that they have usually been written by an English-speaking person trying to use English letters to describe Thai sounds. The task is somewhat difficult, since the written vowels in English are not pronounced consistently. Written English does not differentiate between long and short vowels. This is a major drawback.

Transliteration or Romanization means that we write Thai sounds with symbols other than Thai script. This is known as phonetic writing. The symbols can be of any other alphabet, or international phonetic symbols, where each symbol only denotes one particular sound. Here, we use mainly roman letters to denote a certain sound. However, where there is no relevant letter to express the Thai sound, we use an international phonetic symbol. We have chosen to use in the text the kind of symbols that are easy to understand for an English speaker.

In addition, we give other symbols used by different transliteration systems. The Royal Thai system is also given as a reference. The Royal Thai system is the only official transliteration system in Thailand. It is mainly used for names and road signs. It is not ideal as a transliteration system, since it does not differentiate between long and short vowels, and it usually omits the tone marks. It therefore does not give an accurate description of Thai sounds. Consequently, the Royal Thai system is not used by language schools.

You do not need to learn the Royal Thai system or any other system. They are given only as a reference to show you how complex the transliterations can be. You should first just concentrate on getting all the Thai sounds right as given and transliterated in this book.

Sounds

In this book, we try to explain Thai sounds by also giving you an English word with a similar sound. We shall mainly use General American pronunciation (GA) or Standard British English pronunciation (RP); whichever is appropriate to the similar Thai sound. In addition, we explain the sounds in phonetic terms in order to give you some deeper understanding of how the Thai sounds are produced.

Please do not rely on the English way of spelling Thai sounds. This applies particularly to the vowel sounds. There is no close match between the English sounds and their spelling in the English language. You need to learn a new way to spell sounds using phonetics as described in this book.

As far as the English language is concerned, it is spoken widely by many people with many different accents. Sometimes the accent is so heavy that even a native speaker has difficulty understanding what another person is saying. The main difference between the various accents in English is caused by the variable production of vowel sounds. Consonants are usually produced in more or less the same way. Producing vowel sounds correctly in Thai will be your main challenge in becoming able to speak Thai well enough for Thai people to understand you.

You will need to spend some time and make an effort to understand all the sounds both in theory and practice. After that it is quite easy to learn sentences and simple grammar. Thai grammar is relatively straightforward.

Tones

In addition to being able to pronounce a word correctly, you need to learn to put the right tone into it. In Thai, many words are pronounced the same but with a different tone; a different pitch level. One could say that you need to learn to sing in Thai.

There are five tones: normal or middle tone, low tone, falling tone, high tone and rising tone. Tone is a sound, a pitch level attached to vowel sounds in each word or syllable spoken. Tones are relative since each person has naturally a different starting pitch. Usually men have a lower pitch level than women.

The following diagram is often given to describe the five Thai tones.

The normal tone is pronounced with the normal voice or pitch. The low tone is pronounced lower than the normal voice and the high tone higher than the normal voice. The falling tone starts higher than the normal voice and ends up lower than the normal voice. The rising tone starts lower than the normal voice and ends up higher than the normal voice.

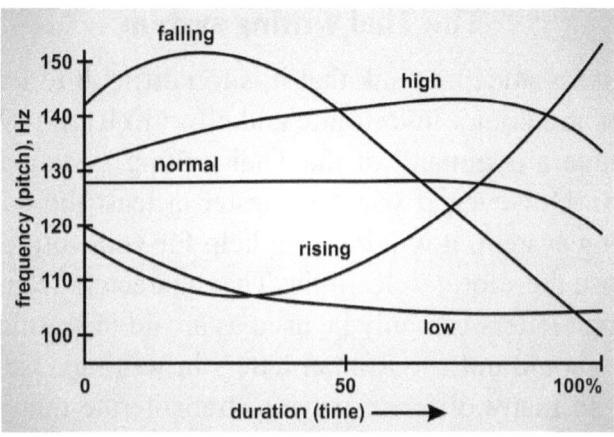

Tone Chart of "Jackson Gandour" (1976)

Tones in Thai language are determined by
- the initial consonant of a word or syllable (Thai consonants are divided into three groups, low, middle and high)
- the vowel length of a word or syllable (vowels are either short or long)
- the final consonant of a word or syllable (the final consonants are either stop sounds or sonorant sounds)
- Thai tone marks (tone marks change the tone of the word)

Later on all terms such as stop sounds and sonorant sounds will be described in detail.

If you wish to be easily understood by Thai people, it is absolutely essential to master Thai sounds and tones well. First, learn all the Thai sounds and tones correctly. It is of no significance how many words and sentences you know if you are not able to pronounce them correctly so that your Thai friends understand you.

The Thai writing system

Many western students think that it is too difficult to learn to read Thai script and do not invest time and effort to learn it. You do not need to have a command of the Thai writing system in order to speak Thai. However, if you can master at least the basics of the Thai writing system, it will be a big help for your future studies. It makes sense therefore, to learn the Thai characters from the beginning. Roman letters can only be used as an aid in learning to speak Thai. You should not use Roman letters in writing Thai sentences. There are so many different ways to transliterate that your effort would be fruitless. Thais would be unlikely to understand what you had written anyway. In Thailand, Roman letters are only used in names and road signs. If you do take the trouble to learn to read and write Thai, Thai people will be very impressed!

Many students spend between 5 and 7 years learning to read Thai well. However, if you take a few minutes every day, with the help of this book, you should be able to learn all the Thai sounds and to read simple Thai text in less than a year.

Ignore the promises presented in some books that within a few months of starting you will be able to communicate extensively with Thai people in their own language. If that does not happen it is not your fault. Empty promises are easy to make, but don't let them dishearten you. Do the "groundwork" first and this will help you to methodically develop your Thai.

Learning Thai: main obstacles

1. Compared to English, the vowel sounds are pronounced quite differently in Thai. You will need to learn new ways to produce correct vowel sounds.

2. Some consonants are pronounced unaspirated at the beginning of the word, while a similar sound is pronounced aspirated in English. See Secret 1.

3. Thai is a tonal language. You need to learn to put tones into words; that is to say to sing Thai. No need to worry: there are only five!

4. To western students the Thai writing system can seem quite complicated. Many therefore give up learning too easily. The system is however, quite logical, and once you put some effort into learning it, you are rewarded.

5. A vast number of words and synonyms are used in special ways in special situations. That can take some effort to learn. Just be sensitive to the Thai culture and you will get there.

Take up the challenge! Do not be discouraged. Thais like to have fun, they hate to be serious. Have fun and smile, too, as you learn the language.

I. Introduction to basic phonetics

Secret 1

In order to master all the Thai sounds it is necessary that you understand some basic phonetics. Phonetics goes deeper than transliteration. It gives you knowledge of how the different sounds of a language are produced. Hence, it will be easier to learn new sounds, which do not exist in the English language.

A. Introduction to basic phonetics

Phonetics: sàtthásàat สัทศาสตร์

Transliteration: kham tháp sàp คำทับศัพท์

All sounds in any language are made by vowels like **i**, **a**, **u**... and consonants like **b**, **c**, **d**... The Thai language is vowel-oriented, which means that vowels play a very important part when making sounds. The English language is more consonant-oriented, meaning that consonants play an important role when producing sounds. Consonants are mainly articulated either by the lips or the tongue. Vowels are mainly articulated by the tongue.

When you speak you send sound waves to the listener's ear. Each person has a unique way of producing sounds. There is, however, a commonly agreed basis as to how the sounds should be produced in each language. You need to learn to produce Thai sounds in such a way that the listener will understand which sound you are forming.

Thai may be the first foreign language you are going to learn. This makes your task very interesting and also challenging. There are many English-speaking people who would like to learn Thai. This book is going to help you on the way by giving you the theoretical knowledge and practical base to produce Thai sounds correctly. It will also point out where you may experience difficulties as an English speaker while learning Thai.

Note that we also give a Thai word for some important terms. You do not need to learn them. However, some serious students may like to know them. The same applies to all written Thai text in this book.

Important consonant qualities

- consonants: pháyanʧáná พยัญชนะ
- aspirated consonant sounds:
  sǐiang pháyanʧáná thîi mii lom เสียง พยัญชนะ ที่ มี ลม
- unaspirated consonant sounds:
  sǐiang pháyanʧáná thîi mâi mii lom เสียง พยัญชนะ ที่ ไม่ มี ลม

Aspirated and unaspirated sounds
When we say that the letter or the sound is aspirated, it means that there is a **clear puff of air** when the sound is produced. An English example would be the letter **p** in the word **Peter**. In unaspirated sounds, there is **no puff of air** when the sound is produced. (However, note that in English, unaspirated sounds do sometimes have a slight puff of air.) An English example would be the letter **p** in the word **spine**. Thai aspirated sounds are more heavily aspirated than similar English sounds, and unaspirated sounds in Thai are made without any puff of air at all. This distinction is very important.

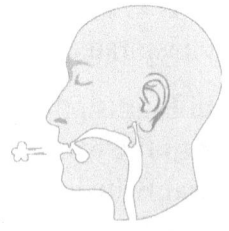
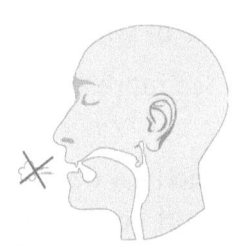

Glottal stop sound

The international symbol for glottal stop is ? which looks like a question mark.

The glottal stop is a consonant or a vowel sound produced while the air flow is stopped in the vocal tract in the throat.

When the consonant stop sounds like **t**, **p** and **k** are made with the glottal stop, the sound is unaspirated without any puff of air. Note that in English these consonant sounds are made aspirated with the puff of air while in Thai they can be made aspirated or unaspirated and hence constitute a different word and a different meaning.

The glottal stop sound is produced when the air flow is first stopped in the glottis by the vocal folds. After that the air is allowed to escape with a plosive, and the sound is made either with the tongue or with the lips.

Many languages make use of the glottal stop.

This is a very important sound as to understand when making the unaspirated stop sounds in Thai.

In English the glottal stop is often used when the last sound **t**, **p** or **k** of the word is not pronounced but stopped in the vocal tract. Several British or American dialects use a glottal stop with end sounds like cat, sip or sack. Cockney English dialect is a very good example of when English sounds are made with a glottal stop.

See more about how to make a glottal stop on the web page:
http://www.youtube.com/watch?v=edxwQK1zBxw&list

The best training for making a glottal stop would be to pronounce short vowel sounds and interrupt the airflow suddenly without closing the lips. Just imagine that somebody jumps out from behind a wall and you are scared to death. You freeze and the sound "uh" comes out of your mouth. You are most likely stopping the sound in your throat, glottis and using the glottal stop sound.

If you understand how to make a glottal stop sound, it will help immensely with your Thai studies. Note however that you cannot ask your Thai friends or even your Thai teachers about the glottal stop unless they are trained in phonetics. They know how to make the sound, but they may not know what the glottal stop is.

In Thai the air for stop sounds like **p**, **t** or **k** can be stopped by the lips, by the tongue or by the vocal folds in the throat. In English the air is stopped usually only by the lips or by the tongue.

Note also that if you pronounce the letter **p** in the English word **Peter** unaspirated, without the puff of air, you will be understood, but considered to be speaking with an accent. In Thai, you would most likely be misunderstood since aspirated and unaspirated sounds at the beginning of a word constitute a different sound and a different word.

Stop and sonorant consonant sounds
- stop consonant sound:
  sǐiang pháyantʃáná yùt เสียง พยัญชนะ หยุด
- sonorant consonant sound:
  sǐiang pháyantʃáná sǐiang kɔ̌ɔng เสียง พยัญชนะ เสียง ก้อง
- closed final sound: kham-taai คำ ตาย
- open final sound: kham-pen คำ เป็น

Stop sounds such as **p, t, d, k**... are made when the air flow is first restricted by stopping it and then released by a plosive. In addition, there are fricative sounds such as **s** and **f**, which are produced by making a narrow channel while the air flow is restricted, which makes a friction. Both stop and fricative sounds form so called "**closed final sounds**" in the Thai tonal system. An example of a closed final sound in English would be the letter **t** in the word cat. The sound is stopped and cannot be prolonged.

Sonorant consonant sounds such as **m, n, w**... are made when the air flow is not restricted. They form so called "**open final sounds**" in the Thai tonal system. An example of an open final sound in English is the letter **m** in the word **him**. The sound is not stopped and can be prolonged indefinitely. Note also that all long vowel sounds in Thai constitute an open end sound like in the English word to **see**. Short vowel sounds in Thai are, however, stopped and therefore make a closed end sound.

As the examples above show there are stop and sonorant consonants in English, but the distinction is not as important as it is in the Thai language. It is very important to distinguish between **closed final sounds** (sometimes also called **stop finals** or **dead endings**) and **open final sounds** (sometimes also called **live endings**) in Thai because of the tonal nature of the language.

Voiced consonant sounds

sĭiang pháyanʧáná sên sĭiang sàn
เสียง พยัญชนะ เส้น เสียง สั้น

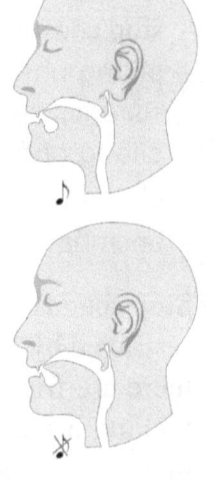

The sound is said to "voiced" when vocal folds are **vibrating** as the sound is produced. An English example would be the letter **g** in the word **g**ate or letter **b** in the word **b**etter. The sound is said to be "unvoiced" when vocal folds are **not vibrating** as the sound is produced. An example of unvoiced consonant sound would be the letter **p** or **t**. Voicing in Thai is somewhat softer than it is in English. In Thai there are only two voiced consonants, **b** and **d**, while in English there is also **g**.

Note that all sonorant consonant sounds such as **m, n, l, r**... in English and Thai are voiced.

Place of articulation

The place of articulation of consonant sounds are lip, teeth, front, middle, back and throat sounds. The phonetic terms for the same are bilabial, dental, alveolar-palatal, veand glottal.

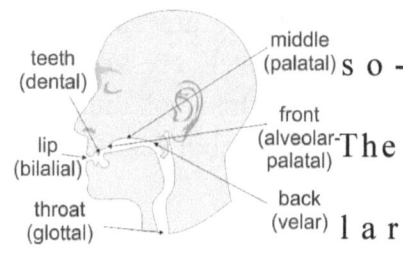

Important vowel qualities

Manner of articulation of vowels

Vowels are very important components in the Thai language – more important than they are in English. In the beginning, we would advise the Thai learner to focus attention on the vowel qualities in spoken Thai. In English, vowels are pronounced with great variety by different groups of English speaking people. Yet, there is not much difficulty in understanding different accents. In Thai, vowels are more clear and precise and can not be blurred into schwa or changed into anything else if you want to be easily understood.

Short or long vowels

The pure vowels are divided into short and long sounds. A short vowel sound always has a long counterpart. The same is not true in English. In English, the quality of a short vowel is often somewhat different from its long counterpart. Hence, it is, in a way, a different sound. In this book, we transliterate a short vowel with one letter and a long vowel with two letters.

Note that in English, there are only 5 vowel letters; **A, E, I, O** and **U**. With these five letters, we should be able to describe about 15–20 different vowel sounds. In English, the same letter can be pronounced one way in one word and another way in another word.

In Thai there are 18 pure vowel sounds, 4 special vowels and 6 diphthongs. Every vowel in Thai denotes a specific clear vowel sound. In this book the transliteration is also based on the principle that one symbol denotes only one sound.

Pure vowels, short and long

	Front	Central	Back
Closed	ì อิ, ii อี	ù อึ, uu อือ	ù อุ, uu อู
Half open	è เอะ, ee เอ	è เออะ, əə เออ	ò โอะ, oo โอ
Open	è แอะ, ɛɛ แอ	à อะ, aa อา	ò เอาะ, ɔɔ ออ

- vowel: sàrà สระ
- short vowel: sàrà sǐiang sân สระ เสียง สั้น
- long vowel: sàrà sǐiang yaau สระ เสียง ยาว
- vowel combinations: sàrà pràsǒm สระ ประสม

Pure vowels and vowel combinations

Pure vowels consist of one single vowel sound – either short or long. The short pure vowel sound in English would be **u**-sound in the word **p**u**t**. The long counterpart is **uu**-sound in the word **s**oo**n**.

When a vowel sound consists of two different sounds, it is called a vowel combination or a diphthong. An English example would be the phonetic sound **ai** as in the word m**y** or in the word l**i**ke. Note that in English the sound is the same but spelling is different. Vowel combinations are usually made from pure vowels.

Closed or open

When we say a vowel sound is **closed**, it means that the tongue is kept close to the roof of the mouth, and the mouth is almost closed. An English example would be the letter **i** in the word happ**y**.

When we say the vowel is **open**, it means that the tongue is kept far away from the roof of the mouth and the mouth is open. An English example would be the letter **a** in the word **s**a**d**. The vowel sounds are divided into closed, half open and open.

Rounded or unrounded
When we say the vowel sound is rounded, it means that the **lips are rounded** when the sound is produced. An English example would be the letter **u** in the word **put**.

When we say the vowel is unrounded, it means that the **lips are unrounded** when the sound is produced. An English example would be the letter **i** in the word **it**.

Place of articulation

Front, middle or back
The places of articulation of vowels can be divided into three locations, front, middle and back.

a) Front vowels are produced in the front of the mouth. An English example would be the letter **i** in the word **it**.

b) Centre vowels are produced in the middle of the mouth. An English example would be the letter **a** in the word **cut**.

c) Back vowels are produced in the back of the mouth. An English example would be the letter **u** in the word **put**.

Note that in Thai the place of articulation is the same for short and long vowels.

In English, the place of articulation is shifted for short and long vowels. For example The long **uu**-sound in the word **soon** is closed, rounded back vowel. The short **u**-sound as in the word **put** is shifted towards the middle. As a native English speaker you are born into the habit and may not realize this. However, when making Thai vowel sounds you need to be aware of where the vowels are produced, since you cannot directly transfer your way of producing English vowels into Thai.

B. Sound exercise 1

(bɛ̀ɛp fɯ̀k-hàt thîi nɯ̀ng แบบ ฝึกหัด ที่ หนึ่ง)

Welcome to the world of Thai sounds
(yin dii tôɔn ráp khâu sùu lôok khɔ̌ɔng sǐiang phaasǎa thai
ยิน ดี ต้อน รับ เข้า สู่ โลก ของ เสียง ภาษาไทย)

I. Introduction to sounds
(kaan nɛ́nam kìiau kàp sàtthásàat การ แนะนำ เกี่ยวกับ สัทศาสตร์)

Aspirated consonant stop sounds
(sǐiang pháyanʧáná yùt thîi mii lom เสียง พยัญชนะ หยุด ที่ มี ลม)

Examples (tuua-yàang ตัว อย่าง)
ph พ phɔɔ, **th** ท thɔɔ, **kh** ค khɔɔ

Unaspirated consonant stop sounds
(sǐiang pháyanʧáná yùt thîi mâi mii lom
เสียง พยัญชนะ หยุด ที่ ไม่ มี ลม)

Examples (tuua-yàang ตัว อย่าง)
p ป pɔɔ, **t** ต tɔɔ, **k** ก kɔɔ

Voiced consonant sounds
(sǐiang pháyanʧáná sên sǐiang sàn เสียง พยัญชนะ เส้น เสียง สั่น)

Examples (tuua-yàang ตัว อย่าง)
b บ bɔɔ, **d** ด dɔɔ

Fricative consonant sounds
(sĭiang pháyanʧáná sìiat sɛ̂ɛk เสียง พยัญชนะ เสียด แทรก)

Examples (tuua-yàang ตัว อย่าง)
f ฟ fɔɔ, s ซ sɔɔ

Sonorant consonant sounds
(sĭiang pháyanʧáná sĭiang kɔ̂ɔng เสียง พยัญชนะ เสียง ก้อง)

Examples (tuua-yàang ตัว อย่าง)
m ม mɔɔ, n น nɔɔ, l ล lɔɔ

Short and long vowels
(sàrà sĭiang sân lέ yaau สระ เสียง สั้น และ ยาว)

Examples (tuua-yàang ตัว อย่าง)

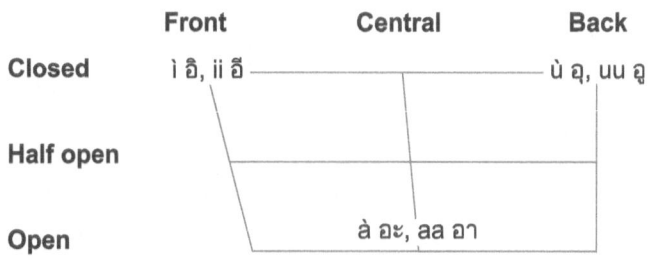

Common expressions (kham thîi ʧái bɔ̀i-bɔ̀i คำ ที่ ใช้ บ่อยๆ)

sàwàtdii   สวัสดี   Hello, Hi, Good bye.

This expression can be used any time of the day. It is often used instead of Good morning, Good afternoon or Good evening.

sàwàtdii khâ   สวัส ดี ค่ะ   (Women say)
sàwàtdii khráp   สวัส ดี ครับ   (Men say)

C. Practical learning tips

You would be well advised to get yourself acquainted with basic phonetics. If you do, you will find that learning Thai becomes much easier. This does not apply only to Thai, but other languages as well.

D. Reading exercise 1

Try to figure out
In English, the following letters are pronounced aspirated at the beginning of a word or syllable. There is a clear puff of air when the sound is made.

Peter, **t**ake and **k**iss

Find an English word for each sound where these three letters are pronounced unaspirated. So that there is no puff of air when the sound is made.

Correct examples are given in the next Secret, page 43.

II. Basic sounds

Secret 2

At the beginning concentrate your efforts on learning the correct Thai sounds. After that you can learn words and how to put them together. If the basic sounds are incorrect then Thai people may not understand your spoken Thai.

To begin with we will study all the **initial sounds** of every consonant and also give the **end sound** of each consonant.

The first group of consonants we shall study is **stop lip sounds p** ป, **b** บ, **ph** พ and **ph** ผ. Stop lip sounds in Thai can be aspirated, unaspirated or voiced. They all have **p** ป as the end sound.

Stop sounds are made in such a way that the air flow is restricted by stopping it and then released with a plosive. Stop sounds form so called "closed final sounds", also called "dead ending" in the Thai tonal system. This is important to know when determining the tone of a word or syllable in Thai script.

In addition, we shall study one **short** vowel sound and it's **long** counterpart in each Secret. Please make the effort to get the vowel sounds right. These vowel sounds can be the **main obstacle** for English speakers in producing Thai sounds and tones correctly.

We will study first the closed vowel sounds, which are produced with the tongue kept as close as possible to the roof of the mouth. The mouth is almost closed.

A. New sounds

I. Consonants

Stop lip sounds bɔɔ บ and pɔɔ ป
Phonetically, these consonant sounds are called unaspirated bilabial stop sounds. Here we call them simply "stop lip sounds". They are produced with both lips. The air is first stopped and then released with a plosive. These two sounds are made in a similar way. The only difference is that bɔɔ บ is voiced, meaning vocal folds are vibrating when the sound is made, while the pɔɔ ป sound is unvoiced and is made with the glottal stop.

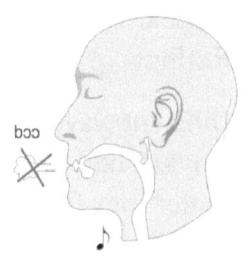

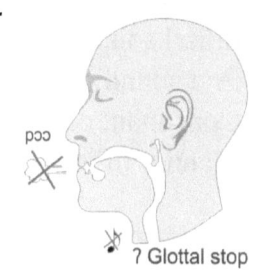

? Glottal stop

bɔɔ บ
Thai name: bai máai ใบ ไม้ leaf
End sound: p ป
Consonant class: Middle
Key: Unaspirated, **voiced**,
                   stop/lip sound

Improve
This **b** บ-sound is made as it sounds in the English word **baby**. If you use the English way, there should be no problems. There is always room for some improvement. The main thing is to improve your pronunciation to a level where Thai people understand you when you use Thai words.

Description
This **b** บ-sound is a voiced and unaspirated stop sound. The place of articulation is bilabial, meaning the sound is produced with the lips. The air flow is first stopped and then released with a plosive. This sound is voiced, meaning the vocal folds are vibrating when you make it. Both in English and Thai, voiced sounds are not aspirated.

Similar English sounds for bɔɔ บ: **b**utter, we**b**, **b**aby
Rating: Good

Different ways to transliterate bɔɔ บ
Royal Thai: b
Other transliterations: b is used by most systems

Summary
Initial sound: bɔɔ บ
End sound: p บ
Consonant class: Middle
Manner of articulation: Unaspirated, unvoiced, stop tongue consonant sound
Place of articulation: Lips (Bilabial)

Note The end sound p บ is pronounced unaspirated at the end of a word or syllable. In Thai, consonants are often pronounced differently depending upon whether they appear at the start or end of a word. This is something that you will soon get used to.

pɔɔ ป
Thai name: plaa ปลา fish
End sound: p บ
Consonant class: Middle
Key: Unaspirated, **unvoiced**, **glottal stop**/lip sound

Improve
This Thai sound is a bit tricky for English speakers, since the letter p in English is pronounced aspirated at the beginning of words like pay. In Thai, the sound p ป is made unaspirated at the beginning of words. In Thai there should be no puff of air when you make this sound. The sound is produced the same way as the previous b บ-sound. The only difference is that b บ-sound is voiced and p ป-sound unvoiced. Learn to make this sound totally unaspirated and unvoiced in the initial position. If you use the English sound as in the word s**p**ot, you are on the way. Try to understand how the

glottal stop sound is made. First stop the air in the glottis and then release it with a plosive from the lips. See more about the glottal stop on page 26.

Perhaps you will need help from a Thai teacher. You will need to break the English habit of producing this sound aspirated at the beginning of the word.

Description

This **p** ป-sound is an unvoiced and unaspirated glottal stop sound. The place of articulation is glottal bilabial, meaning the sound is produced with the lips and with the glottal stop. The air flow is first stopped and then released with a plosive.

Note English speakers tend to pronounce stop consonants at the beginning of a word either voiced as **b** or aspirated as **ph**. Some transliterations use **bp**, and say that this sound is between **b** and **p**. Well, **b** is voiced as in the English word **baby** and **p** is aspirated as in the English word **Peter**. The Thai sound **p** ป is neither voiced nor aspirated. It is an unaspirated glottal stop sound.

If you pronounce **p** unaspirated, then you will be making the sound, **p** ป. Or if you compare this sound with the **b** บ-sound, the key is to make it **unvoiced** and you will then come to the same sound, **p** ป.

As an aid to correct sound production, just put your hand in front of your mouth and feel. If there is still a puff of air coming out of your mouth, the sound is aspirated and is incorrect. With a little practice you will get it right. First try **ph** as in the English word **Peter** and note that there is a clear puff of air coming from your mouth. Then learn to say unaspirated **p** ป correctly with no puff of air.

English speakers listening to Thai tend to hear a **b** บ-sound at the beginning of words when in fact **p** ป is being used. Train your ear by listening closely to Thai native speakers to hear when the unaspirated and unvoiced stop sound **p** ป is used.

Similar English sounds for ปอ ป: **sp**ot, **sp**eak, **sp**ine
Rating: Not very good

Different ways to transliterate ปอ ป
Royal Thai: p
Other transliterations: p, bp

Summary
Initial sound: ปอ ป
End sound: p ป
Consonant class: Middle
Manner of articulation: Unvoiced, unaspirated stop consonant
Place of articulation: Glottal, lips (Bilabial)

2. Vowels

Closed front vowels ิ อิ and ีี อี

	Front	Central	Back
Closed	ิ อิ, ีี อี	ึ อึ, ืื อือ	ุ อุ, ูู อู
Half open	เิะ เอะ, เee เอ	เิะ เออะ, ออ เออ	โิะ โอะ, oo โอ
Open	แิะ แอะ, แεε แอ	อะ อะ, aa อา	เิาะ เอาะ, ออ ออ

Improve
Please learn to separate the short ิ อิ-sound from its long counterpart ีี อี.

Short ิ อิ
If you produce the short sound like in the English word ha**pp**y, you are quite close.

Long ii อี-sound

The long ii อี-sound is quite close to the English sound in the word see. You should be able to use the English sound with no problems. Check with a native speaker or Thai teacher that you are making these two sounds correctly.

Description

ĭ อิ and ii อี-sounds are closed, unrounded front vowels. When you produce these sounds, lips are unrounded as if you were smiling. The place of articulation is in the front part of the mouth. Closed means that the tongue is kept as close as possible to the roof of the mouth, and that the mouth is almost closed.

Note A single ĭ อิ-sound as in the word sit is short. The long ii อี-sound written with two ii letters as in the English word meat. The same applies to all vowels. One vowel letter here denotes a short sound and two vowel letters a long sound. In English, the same letter can be pronounced one way in a certain word and a different way in another word. Good examples are the words; sit, mite and said, where the letter i is pronounced in three different ways.

Similar English sounds for short ĭ อิ: happy, think, sit
Rating: Good
Similar English sounds for long ii อี: see, meat, teach
Rating: Good

Different ways to transliterate
Short ĭ อิ
Royal Thai: i
Other transliterations: i, y, ee!, ĭ

Long ii อี
Royal Thai: i
Other transliterations: i, ii, i:, ee

Summary
Vowel length: Short ì อิ and long ii อี
Manner of articulation: Closed, unrounded vowel sound
Place of articulation: Front

Note A reminder: You do **not need to learn** different ways to transliterate sounds. Examples are only given here as a reference to show you how complicated it can be. This list of transliterations is far from complete!

The Royal Thai system does not differentiate between short and long vowel sounds.

B. Sound exercise 2
(bɛ̀ɛp fɯ̀k-hàt thîi sɔ̌ɔng แบบ ฝึกหัด ที่ สอง)

b บ bɔɔ
p ป pɔɔ

ì อิ, ii อี

Examples (tuua-yàang ตัว อย่าง)
bì   บิ   to break off
bìip   บีบ   to squeeze, to press

pìt   ปิด   to close
pìip   ปีบ   cork tree

Repeating sounds learned so far (phûut sám พูด ซ้ำ)
bin   บิน   to fly
biin   บีน   only a sound, no meaning

pìn   ปิ่น   hairpin
pìi   ปี่   flute

Common expressions (kham thîi tʃái bɔ̀i-bɔ̀i คำ ที่ใช้ บ่อยๆ)

sàbaai dii mái	สบาย ดี ไหม	How are you?
sàbaai dii khâ	สบาย ดี ค่ะ	I am fine, thank you. (woman)
sàbaai dii khráp	สบาย ดี ครับ	I am fine, thank you. (man)
sàbaai sàbaai	สบาย สบาย	Quite okay.

C. Practical learning tips

In order to learn a new language like Thai, we need to know the sounds both in theory and in practice. If you only listen and try to imitate, there is a tendency that you will hear what you are accustomed to hearing, and therefore will not be able to reproduce the sound correctly. Correct tongue and lip positions are very important. We are no longer children, who can learn a language very quickly only by imitating. You have been speaking your own language for many years, and it has penetrated deeply into your mind and consciousness.

D. Reading exercise 2

Answers from the reading exercise 1 page 34
Examples would be: **p** as in the word "spin", **t** as in the word "stone" and **k** as in "skin". These letters are in the middle of a word or syllable. They are pronounced unaspirated or only slightly aspirated in English.

In Thai, the same letters can be unaspirated also at the beginning of the word, while in English, they are always aspirated. You need to recognise the difference between aspirated and unaspirated sounds at the beginning of the word. In Thai, the distinction between aspirated and unaspirated sounds is clear and very important.

Reading exercise

Try to figure out how the following word is pronounced in Thai:
ปู

The correct transliteration is given in the next Secret, page 51.

 You may like to skip these sections (Ds) now, and come back to them later when you are ready to learn the Thai script and tonal system. In order to learn sounds, you don't need to master the Thai writing system. We would however, recommend starting to learn the Thai script right from the start. That way your understanding becomes much deeper than if you only rely on transliterated text. You will also learn the tone rules much faster. The only way to learn to read Thai is to start reading individual words and then build up to read phrases and sentences.

Secret 3

At the beginning when learning Thai you need to pay attention to whether a vowel is short and long. The vowels should sound the same, only the duration of the sound is different. The same is not true in English, where the long counterpart of a short vowel can change the quality of the sound.

A. New sounds

I. Consonants

Stop lip sounds **phɔɔ** พ and **phɔ̌ɔ** ผ
Phonetically, these consonant sounds are called unvoiced aspirated bilabial stop sounds. We call them simply "stop lip sounds" since they are made by using both lips, lower and upper. Both of these sounds are made the same way. The only difference is that **phɔɔ** พ belongs to the low consonant group and **phɔ̌ɔ** ผ to the high group. Hence, the tone is different.

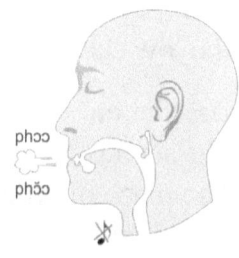

End sound

We also give the end sound of the same consonant. This is very important in Thai, since the end sound also plays a role in determining the tone of a word or syllable.

phɔɔ พ
Thai name: **phaan** พาน tray
End sound: **p** ป
Consonant class: Low

phɔ̌ɔ ผ
Thai name: **phûng** ผึ้ง bee
End sound: **p** ป
Consonant class: High

Key: **Aspirated**, unvoiced, stop/lip sound

Improve
If you use the English sound as in the word **pretty**, there should be no problem. However, make this sound, even more aspirated than the English sound. The **phɔ̌ɔ** ผ-sound is made exactly the same way as **phɔɔ** พ-sound. It belongs, however, to the high consonant group which affects the tone differently. You need to learn to pronounce the high class consonants here with the "rising tone" and the low class consonants with the "normal tone". More on this later.

Description
The sounds **phɔɔ** พ and **phɔ̌ɔ** ผ are unvoiced, aspirated stop sounds. The place of articulation is bilabial, meaning that the sound is produced with the lips. The air flow is first stopped and then released with a plosive.

Note This is quite an easy sound for English speakers, since the English letter **p** is pronounced aspirated at the beginning of a word. Aspiration means that there is a puff of air released when the sound is pronounced. The letter **h** is a good example of aspiration. The aspiration in Thai can be even stronger than in English. The distinction between aspirated and unaspirated sounds in Thai is important and must be made clearly.

Similar English sounds for **phɔɔ** พ and **phɔ̌ɔ** ผ: **pretty, pay, put**

Rating: Good

Different ways to transliterate **phɔɔ** พ and **phɔ̌ɔ** ผ
Royal Thai: ph
Other transliterations: ph, p

Summary
Initial sound: **phɔɔ** พ and **phɔ̌ɔ** ผ
End sound: **p** ป
Consonant class: Low and high
Manner of articulation: Unvoiced, aspirated stop consonant sounds
Place of articulation: Lips (Bilabial)

Note The end sound **p** ป is pronounced unaspirated at the end of a word or syllable. However, the high class consonant **phɔ̌ɔ** ผ does not appear as an end sound.

2. Vowels

Closed central unrounded vowel sounds อึ and อือ

	Front	Central	Back
Closed	i อิ, ii อี	อึ, อือ	u อุ, uu อู
Half open	e เอะ, ee เอ	ə เออะ, əə เออ	o โอะ, oo โอ
Open	ɛ แอะ, ɛɛ แอ	a อะ, aa อา	ɔ เอาะ, ɔɔ ออ

Improve
Learn to separate the short อึ-sound from its long counterpart อือ.

Short ึ อึ-sound

The short ึ อึ-sound is difficult for English speakers. However, some English speakers seem to use a similar sound to the Thai sound ึ อึ in words like sh**ou**ld and g**oo**d. Other English speakers use the ุ อุ-sound as in the word l**oo**k. You will most likely need help from a native Thai teacher to get this sound right.

Practice this sound by first putting your lips as if you were producing the ิ อิ-sound as in the word **i**t, then say a ุ อุ-sound with unrounded lips as in the word l**oo**k. What you produce will come close to the short ึ อึ-sound. The sound is produced in the centre of the mouth. Thai teachers often say that you should produce this sound with a smile and only with the tongue. The lips are not used at all and remain unrounded.

Long ืื อือ-sound

Long ืื อือ-sound does not exist in Standard English in its pure form. This sound is made the same way as the previous short sound but the duration of the sound is longer. Some English speakers seem to use a similar ืื อือ-sound in the words like c**u**te and r**u**de. Other English speakers use the **uu** อู-sound as in the word c**oo**l. In English, there seem to be no problems whether one pronounces the above words one way or the other. It depends on the speaker. Some Australian, New Zealand and Scottish English speakers use the ืื อือ-sound, which is close to the Thai sound.

Description

These sounds, the short ึ อึ and the long ืื อือ are closed, unrounded middle vowels. When you produce these sounds, lips are unrounded as if you were smiling. The place of articulation is in the 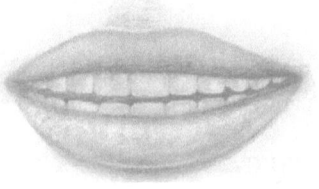 middle part of the mouth. Closed means that the tongue is kept as close as possible to the roof of the mouth, and the mouth is almost closed.

Note Sometimes this sound is also transliterated as ɨ. ɨ denotes the same sound and is phonetically more precise. We, however, use the phonetic symbol ʉ, since it is already used by many other transliterations and is visually more easily understood. It is often said that there is no comparable sound in English. This is not quite true, since some English speakers, even in England and the USA, seem to use a similar sound with words like c**ou**ld, sh**ou**ld, g**oo**d, c**u**te, f**ew** and r**u**de. Others pronounce the same sound differently.

Similar English sounds for short ʉ อึ: sh**ou**ld, g**oo**d, w**ou**ld
Rating: Not very good
Similar English sounds for long ʉʉ อือ: c**u**te, f**ew**, r**u**de
Rating: Not very good

Different ways to transliterate
Short ʉ อึ
Royal Thai: ue
Other transliterations: ʉ, ue, eu, ue!, ɯ, ɨ

Long ʉʉ อือ
Royal Thai: ue
Other transliterations: ʉʉ, eu, ue:, ɯ:, ɨɨ

Summary
Vowel length: Short ʉ อึ and long ʉʉ อือ
Manner of articulation: Closed unrounded vowel sounds
Place of articulation: Central

B. Sound exercise 3

(bɛ̀ɛp fùk-hàt thîi sǎam แบบ ฝึก หัด ที่ สาม)

ph พ phɔɔ
ph ผ phɔ̌ɔ

ึ อึ, ืe อือ

Examples (tuua-yàang ตัว อย่าง)
phɨng   พึ่ง   to depend on
phɨɨt   พืช   plant

phɨ̀ng   ผึ่ง   to dry, to expose
phɨ̀ɨn   ผื่น   prickly heat

Repeating sounds learned so far (phûut sám พูด ซ้ำ)
phin   พิณ   Indian lute
piin   ปีน   to climb

phít   พิษ   poison
phíit   พีช   peach

bɨng   บึ้ง   to be serious
pɨ̀ɨn   ปื้น   eruption on the skin

phɨ̂ng   ผึ้ง   bee
phɨ̀ɨn   ผืน   sheet

Common expressions (kham thîi ʧái bɔ̀i-bɔ̀i คำ ที่ ใช้ บ่อยๆ)

wan-níi rɔ́ɔn mâak   วัน นี้ ร้อน มาก   Today is very hot.
wan-níi nǎau mâak   วัน นี้ หนาว มาก   Today is very cold.
fǒn tòk   ฝน ตก   It is raining.

C. Practical learning tips

While learning Thai it would be good if you could forget the English way of spelling vowels altogether, and learn a new phonetic way as shown in this book. That way, you will learn more quickly to pronounce the Thai vowel sounds more accurately.

Note also that short and long English vowel sounds are not easy to describe accurately even if you are a linguist. There are many different accents, which use somewhat different vowel sounds for the same word. English vowel sounds can only give you a superficial understanding of how the Thai vowel sounds are pronounced.

D. Reading exercise 3

Answers from the reading exercise 2 page 44
pii   ปี   year

Consonant class: middle
End sound: **Open**
Vowel length: Long
Tone: Normal

Tone rule I for the normal tone
When a word or syllable starts with a **low** or **middle class** consonant, and the word ends with an **open final sound**, then the tone is **normal**.

The word starts with the **middle** class consonant **p** ป, which is pronounced unaspirated. There is not any puff of air when the sound is produced. The long ii อี-vowel, which sounds as in the English word m**ea**t, is written above the consonant **p** ป. The word ends with the long vowel sound ii อี, which makes an **open** final sound.

Tone

The tone is **normal**, since the word starts with a **middle** class consonant and ends with an **open** sound.

Note When there is no tone mark, and the word ends with an open sound, there are only two possible tones: The **normal** tone with **low** and **middle** class consonants and the **rising** tone for the **high** class consonant.

See more about end sounds in Secret number 19 and about tone rules in the 20th Secret.

Reading exercise

Try to figure out how the following word is pronounced in Thai:

The correct transliteration is given in the next Secret, page 59.

Secret 4

There are three different types of consonant sounds in Thai. These are stop sounds, fricative sounds and sonorant sounds. The same is true in English, but how to produce and use these sounds differs. Moreover, this kind of classification is more important in Thai because of the tonal nature of the language.

The second group of sounds are **fricative lip-teeth sounds f ฟ and f ฝ**.

Fricative sounds are produced by making a narrow channel while the air flow is restricted, this makes a friction. Both stop and fricative sounds form so called "stop final sounds" or "dead endings" in the Thai tonal system.

A. New sounds

I. Consonants

Fricative lip-teeth sounds fɔɔ ฟ and fɔ̌ɔ ฝ
Phonetically, these consonant sounds are called unvoiced, unaspirated, labiodental fricative sounds. We call them simply "fricative lip-teeth sounds", since these sounds are articulated with the lower lip and upper teeth. The only difference between these two sounds is that the fɔɔ ฟ-sound belongs to the low class consonant group and the fɔ̌ɔ ฝ-sound to the high class consonant group, they hence constitute a different tone.

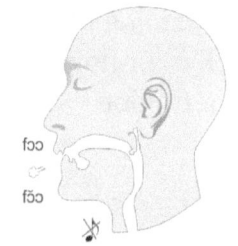

Fricative lip-teeth sounds f ฟ, f ฝ

The fricative sounds are produced by constricting the air flow through a narrow channel. The turbulence of air makes **a friction**.

fɔɔ ฟ
Thai name: fan ฟัน teeth
End sound: p บ
Consonant class: Low

fɔ̌ɔ ฝ
Thai name: fǎa ฝา lid, cover
End sound: p บ
Consonant class: High

Key: Unaspirated, unvoiced, **fricative**/lip-teeth sounds

Improve
If you use the English sound as in the word **ph**oto, that will be fine. The fɔɔ ฟ-sound is pronounced with the normal tone. The fɔ̌ɔ ฝ-sound is produced exactly the same way as the previous sound. However, the fɔ̌ɔ ฝ-sound belongs to the high class consonant group, and is pronounced using the rising tone.

Description
These fɔɔ ฟ and fɔ̌ɔ ฝ-sounds are unvoiced and unaspirated, fricative consonant sounds. The place of articulation is labiodental, meaning the sound is produced with the lower lip and upper teeth. The air flow is restricted by making a narrow channel, which makes a friction.

Fricative lip-teeth sounds f ฟ, f ฝ

Note Another labiodental sound in English is the letter **v** as in the word **v**ote. The difference between **f** and **v** is that the **f**-sound is an unvoiced fricative consonant sound and the **v**-sound is voiced consonant sound. The voiced **v**-sound, however, does not exist in Thai. The only labiodental sound in Thai is the **f**-sound.

English sounds for fɔɔ ฟ and fɔ̌ɔ ฝ: **ph**oto, o**ff**, **f**ool
Rating: Good

Different ways to transliterate fɔɔ ฟ and fɔ̌ɔ ฝ
Royal Thai: f
Other transliterations: f is used by most of the transliteration systems

Summary
Initial sound: fɔɔ ฟ and fɔ̌ɔ ฝ
End sound: p บ
Consonant class: Low and high
Manner of articulation: Unvoiced unaspirated fricative consonant sounds
Place of articulation: Lip-teeth (Labiodental)

Note p บ is pronounced unaspirated at the end of a word or syllable. You must get used to the fact that in Thai end sounds are pronounced differently compared to the same initial sounds. The high class consonant fɔ̌ɔ ฝ does not appear as an end sound at all.

Consonants are divided into three groups, **low**, **medium** and **high**. The consonant group affects the tone of the word. There are fewer consonants in the middle and high class than in the low class group. This classification is used to determine the tone in the Thai writing system. If you decide to learn the Thai script, you will need to know the class of a consonant in order to determine the right tone.

2. Vowels

Closed back vowel sounds ù อุ and uu อู

	Front	Central	Back
Closed	ì อิ, ii อี ———	ǜ อึ, ǚǚ อือ ———	ù อุ, uu อู
Half open	è เอะ, ee เอ	è เออะ, əə เออ	ò โอะ, oo โอ
Open	ɛ̀ แอะ, ɛɛ แอ	à อะ, aa อา	ɔ̀ เอาะ, ɔɔ ออ

Improve
Learn to separate the short **ù** อุ-sound from its long counterpart **uu** อู.

Short ù อุ-sound
If you use the English sound as in the word l**oo**k for the short **ù** อุ-sound, you will be quite close.

Note that the English short **ù** อุ tends to be pronounced a bit differently by different English speakers. Some English speakers even seem to use another Thai sound **ǜ** อึ, which we learned in the previous section, in words like sh**ou**ld or c**ou**ld. Do not mix up these two Thai sounds **ù** อุ and **ǜ** อึ. The distinction between the two is important.

Long uu อู-sound
If you use the English sound as in the words s**oo**n or c**oo**l for the long **uu** อู-sound, you are quite close. You may like to ask your native Thai teacher whether you produce these two sounds exactly right.

Note that the long English **uu** ดู-sound is sometimes pronounced differently by different English speakers. Some may use a version similar to the Thai sound, ~~uu~~ อือ. This happens often with words like n**ew**, d**ew**, g**oo**d, **tw**o. Do not mix up these two sounds **uu** ดู and ~~uu~~ อือ. In Thai, they are clearly different sounds. In English, the distinction is not so clear.

Description
Lips are rounded, and the place of articulation is at the back part of the mouth. Closed means that the tongue is kept as close as possible to the roof of the mouth.

Similar English sounds for short **ù** ดุ:
l**oo**k, p**u**t, f**oo**t
Rating: Quite good, but pay attention
Similar English sounds for long **uu** ดู: c**oo**l, s**oo**n, d**o**
Rating: Quite good, but pay attention

Different ways to transliterate
Short **ù** ดุ
Royal Thai: u
Other transliterations: u, OO, o, o͡o, u!

Long **uu** ดู
Royal Thai: u
Other transliterations: uu, u, u:, o, o:, oo, uh,

Summary
Vowel length: Short **ù** ดุ and long **uu** ดู
Manner of articulation: Closed, rounded vowel sounds
Place of articulation: Back

B. Sound exercise 4

(bὲɛp fɯ̀k-hàt thîi sìi แบบ ฝึก หัด ที่ สี่)

f ฟ fɔɔ
f ฝ fɔ̌ɔ

ɯ̀ อุ, ɯɯ อู

Examples (tuua-yàang ตัว อย่าง)
fun	ฟุน	(only a sound, no meaning)
fuu	ฟู	to swell, to rise
fùn	ฝุ่น	dust
fǔung	ฝูง	group, flock

Repeating sounds learned so far (phûut sám พูด ซ้ำ)
phin	ภินท์	to destroy (not used much)
plìk	ปีก	wing
fɯ̀k	ฝึก	to practice
fɯɯn	ฟืน	firewood
pù	ปุ	to repair
pùu	ปู่	grandfather
bun	บุญ	merit
phuun	พูน	to pile up

Common expressions (kham thîi ʧái bɔ̀i-bɔ̀i คำ ที่ใช้ บ่อยๆ)
an-níi àrai	อัน นี้ อะไร	What is this?
an-níi thâu-rài	อัน นี้ เท่า ไหร่	How much is that?
dii mái	ดี ไหม	Is it good?
dii mâak	ดี มาก	Very good!

C. Practical learning tips

Royal Thai is the only official transliteration system in use. It is mainly used for names and road signs in Thailand. However, it has several shortcomings in describing Thai sounds accurately. For instance, it does not differentiate between short and long vowels. It usually also omits tone marks. It is therefore not often used in language schools or in Thai learning books.

The symbols and letters we have chosen to use in this book describe Thai sounds more accurately than many other systems. They should not be too difficult to learn.

Here, we do not follow any Thai alphabetic order, but take each sound one after another depending on how and where they are produced in the mouth. The alphabetic order, which is given at the end of the book, is needed mainly when you look up words in a dictionary.

D. Reading exercise 4

Answers from the reading exercise 3 page 52
phii พี fat

Consonant class: Low
End sound: **Open**
Vowel length: Long
Tone: Normal

Tone rule for the normal tone
When a word starts with a **low** or **middle class** consonant, and when a word ends with an **open final sound**, the tone is **normal**.

phii พี

The word starts with the **low** class consonant **ph** พ, which is pronounced strongly aspirated as in the English word **P**eter. There is a clear puff of air when the sound is produced. The long vowel sound **ii** อี as in the English word m**ea**t is written on the top of the consonant **ph** พ. The word ends with the long vowel sound **ii** อี, which makes an **open** final sound.

Tone

The tone is **normal**, since the word starts with a **low** class consonant and ends with an **open** final sound, long vowel.

Note When there is no tone mark, and when the word ends with an open sound, it can only have two tones, a **normal** tone with **low** and **middle** class consonants and a **rising** tone with a high class consonant.

See more about end sounds in Secret number 19 and about tone rules in the 20th Secret.

Reading exercise

Try to figure out how the following word is pronounced in Thai:

ผี

The correct transliteration is given in the next Secret, page 67.

Secret 5

*Stop sounds in Thai can be **aspirated** or **unaspirated** at the beginning of a word or syllable. However, they are never aspirated at the end of a word or syllable. Therefore, all aspirated stop sounds merge into unaspirated sounds when they form an end sound. In English, stop sounds are always aspirated at the beginning of a word and also often partially at the end.*

The next group of sounds is **stop teeth sounds th** ท, **th** ถ, **t** ต and **d** ด. Note that all stop teeth sounds have **t** ต as the end sound.

A. New sounds

I. Consonants

Stop teeth sounds thɔɔ ท and thɔ̌ɔ ถ
Phonetically, these consonant sounds are called unvoiced, alveolar stops sounds. We call them simply "stop teeth sounds", since they are made by putting the blade of the tongue clearly behind the upper teeth towards the alveolar ridge. The air is first stopped with the tongue and then released with a plosive. These two sounds are made in exactly the same way. The sound is heavily aspirated. The only difference between the two is that the thɔɔ ท-sound belongs to the low class consonant group, and the thɔ̌ɔ ถ-sound to the high class consonant group. They thus produce a different tone.

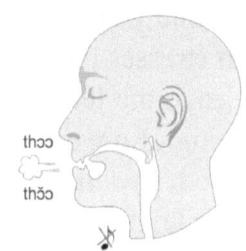

Please note that these sounds are not, however, the same as the English teeth sounds such as the **th**-sound in the English word tee**th** or **th**is. These English sounds are not stop but fricative sounds, and the tongue is placed under the upper teeth rather than behind.

thɔɔ ท
Thai name: tháhǎan ทหาร soldier
End sound: t ต
Consonant class: Low

thǔɔ ถ
Thai name: thǔng ถุง bag
End sound: tɔɔ ต
Consonant class: High

Key: **Aspirated**, unvoiced, stop/tongue-teeth sound

Improve

English speakers do not usually have problems with this sound **thɔɔ** ท. It is similar to the sound in the English word **two**. Just make this sound, but with an even stronger aspiration.

First stop the airflow by putting the blade of you tongue behind the upper teeth, touching the alveolar ridge and then release the sound with a plosive. We transliterate this sound with **th**. The letter **h** stresses the fact that the sound is aspirated. Some transliterations leave the letter **h** out, since the English **t** is aspirated at the beginning of a word or syllable. The tongue is resting against the upper teeth towards the alveolar ridge, and the sound is made with the blade of the tongue.

Be aware of the fact that in Thai, these two sounds are made exactly the same way. The **thɔɔ** ท-sound belongs to the low consonant group and is pronounced with the normal tone. The **thǔɔ** ถ-sound belongs to the high consonant group and is pronounced with the rising tone.

Description

These **thɔɔ** ท and **thɔ̌ɔ** ถ-sounds are unvoiced and aspirated stop sounds. The place of articulation is alveolar; meaning that the blade of the tongue is placed behind the upper teeth touching the front part of the alveolar ridge. The air flow is first stopped with the tongue and then released with a plosive.

Similar English sounds for **thɔɔ** ท and **thɔ̌ɔ** ถ: **t**wo, **t**ake, **t**urn
Rating: Good

Different ways to transliterate **thɔɔ** ท and **thɔ̌ɔ** ถ
Royal Thai: th
Other transliterations: th, t

Summary
Initial sound: **thɔɔ** ท and **thɔ̌ɔ** ถ
End sound: **t** ต
Consonant class: Low and high
Manner of articulation: Aspirated, unvoiced, stop/tongue
                          consonant sounds
Place of articulation: Teeth (Alveolar)

Note The end sound **t** ต is pronounced unaspirated at the end of a word or syllable. You must get used to the fact that in Thai consonants are pronounced differently depending whether they appear at the start or the end of a word or syllable.

2. Vowels

Half open front vowel sounds è เอะ and ee เอ

	Front	Central	Back
Closed	ì อิ, ii อี	ǹ อึ, ʉʉ อือ	ù อุ, uu อู
Half open	è เอะ, ee เอ	ə̀ เออะ, əə เออ	ò โอะ, oo โอ
Open	ὲ แอะ, εε แอ	à อะ, aa อา	ɔ̀ เอาะ, ɔɔ ออ

Improve
Learn to separate the short **è** เอะ-sound from its long counterpart **ee** เอ.

Short è เอะ-sound
The short **è** เอะ-sound does not exist in Standard English in its pure form. English speakers tend to make this sound more open than Thai people do. Hence, it becomes quite close to another sound, which is transliterated as **ε**. An English example would be the word cat. However, Australian and New Zealand English speakers seem to have this sound closer to the Thai sound as in the word p**e**t.

If you use the Standard English sound as in the word p**e**t for the short **è** เอะ-sound, you are on the way. Ask your native Thai teacher to correct your pronunciation in order to learn to get this sound right.

Long ee เอ-sound
The long **ee** เอ-sound does not exist in Standard English in its pure form. If you use the English sound as in the word s**ai**l without the **i**-sound for the long **ee** เอ-sound, you are on the way. The long **ee** เอ-sound is exactly the same as the short **è** เอะ-sound but longer. Or if you pronounce the word p**a**le like p**ee**il without the **i**-sound, you are close to this Thai sound. Some Welsh and Irish speakers of

English seem to have this sound quite close in words like gre**a**t and d**a**te. Ask a native Thai teacher to check your pronunciation so that you make this sound long and correct.

Description

These vowels are pronounced in the front of the mouth, with the mouth half open. The lips are unrounded. Be aware of the fact that in Thai, the long and short vowels are pronounced the same, only the duration is different. The same does not apply to English. In English, the length of the vowel often changes the quality of the sound.

Similar English sounds for short **è** เอะ: p**e**t, s**ai**d, br**ea**d
Rating: Quite good, but pay attention
Similar English words for long **ee** เอ: p**a**le, p**ai**nt, s**ai**l
Rating: Quite good, but pay attention

Different ways to transliterate
Short **è** เอะ
Royal Thai: e
Other transliterations: e, e!, ê

Long **ee** เอ
Royal Thai: e
Other transliterations: ee, e, e: ay

Note Be aware that when you read some Thai learning books, it is often difficult to figure out which sound the particular transliteration is describing. This is mainly because Thai vowel sounds are being described with English letters.

The English language is not consistent with regard to spelling. That is to say, sounds in the English language when written are not consistently spelled. In this book, we use letters and symbols to denote Thai sounds consistently, to avoid misunderstanding. Once you know all the Thai sounds well, you won't be easily mislead by different transliteration systems.

Summary
Vowel length: Short è เอะ and long ee เอ
Manner of articulation: Half open, unrounded vowel sounds
Place of articulation: Front

B. Sound exercise 5

(bɛ̀ɛp fɨ̀k-hàt thîi hâa แบบ ฝึก หัด ที่ ห้า)

th ท thɔɔ
th ถ thɔ̌ɔ

è เอะ, ee เอ

Examples (tuua-yàang ตัว อย่าง)
| thennít | เทนนิส | tennis |
| thee | เท | to pour |

| thét | เท็จ | false, incorrect |
| thêet | เทศ | foreign |

Repeating sounds learned so far (phûut sám พูด ซ้ำ)
| thíp | ทิป | tip |
| thìip | ถีบ | to shove away |

| thɨ̀k | ถึก | wild and strong |
| thɨ̌ɨ | ถือ | to carry |

| pen | เป็น | to be |
| pheen | เพล | lunch time (monk) |

| pèt | เป็ด | duck |
| thêep | เทพ | god, divine being |

Common expressions (kham thîi tʃái bɔ̀i-bɔ̀i คำ ที่ ใช้ บ่อยๆ)

khun phûut thai kèng	คุณ พูดไทย เก่ง	You speak Thai very well.
khɔ̀ɔp-khun khâ	ขอบ คุณ ค่ะ	Thank you. (women)
khɔ̀ɔp-khun khráp	ขอบ คุณ ครับ	Thank you. (men)
khɔ̀ɔp-khun mâak	ขอบ คุณ มาก	Thank you very much.
mâi kèng rɔ̀ɔk	ไม่ เก่ง หรอก	Not very well at all.

C. Practical learning tips

Don't worry too much about the tones in the beginning, even though they are an essential part of the Thai language. Before you can learn tones, you need to know how the word is pronounced without putting the right tone into it.

We give a rating for each sound that implies how well the Standard British English or General American English sounds can be used while speaking Thai. The rating given here is only an indication and should not be taken as an absolute truth. Note also that the English language is spoken widely with different accents, and the sounds, particularly the vowel sounds, differ a lot depending on who uses the language and where.

D. Reading exercise 5

Answers from the reading exercise 4 page 60
phǐi   ผี   ghost

Consonant class: High
End sound: **Open**
Vowel length: Long
Tone: Rising

Tone rule for the rising tone
When the word starts with a **high class consonant** and the word or the syllable ends with an **open** final sound, the tone is **rising**. The vowel can be either short or long.

phǐi ผี
The word starts with the **high** class consonant **ph** ผ, which is pronounced strongly aspirated as in the English word **Peter**. There is a clear puff of air when the sound is produced. The long **ii** อี -vowel sound as in the English word m**ea**t is written on the top of the consonant **ph** ผ. The word ends with the long vowel sound **ii** อี, which makes an **open** final sound.

Tone
The tone is **rising**, since the word starts with a **high** class consonant and ends with an **open** sound.

See more about end sounds in Secret number 19, and about tone rules in the 20th Secret.

Note When there is no tone mark and the final sound is **open**, a **rising** tone can only be constituted by a high class consonant.

Reading exercise

Try to figure out how the following words are pronounced in Thai:

ปีก

ถูก

The correct transliterations are given in the next Secret, page 77.

Secret 6

There are fewer sounds than alphabet characters in the Thai language. Hence, many similar consonant sounds are denoted by different consonant characters. In Thai, a consonant can be pronounced differently depending on whether it appears at the beginning or end of a word or syllable. There are also fewer end sounds than initial sounds in Thai.

End sounds can be different from initial sounds, because an end sound is never aspirated. The end sound is the sound that a consonant makes when it appears at the end of a syllable or word.

There are 20 Thai consonant sounds denoted by the 28 most common consonants characters. In Thai, all these consonants can however make only 8 end sounds.

The Thai language has 9 short and 9 long pure vowels and 6 so called diphthongs or vowel combinations. In addition, there are 4 special vowels. Hence, the Thai vowel list consists of 28 vowel sounds altogether. Every vowel sound is clearly marked by a specific symbol.

A. New sounds

I. Consonants

Stop teeth sounds dɔɔ ด and tɔɔ ต
Phonetically, these two consonant sounds are called **voiced and unvoiced unaspirated alveolar stop** sounds. We call them "stop teeth sounds", since they are made by putting the front of the tongue behind the front teeth against the alveolar ridge. The dɔɔ ด-sound is clearly **voiced**, meaning the vocal folds are vibrating, and the tɔɔ ต-sound is clearly **unvoiced** and **unaspirated**, meaning there is no puff of air when you make the sound.

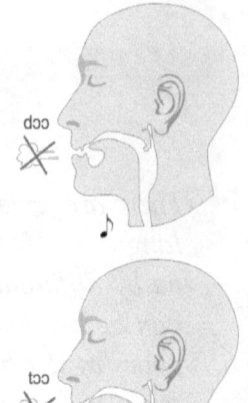

dɔɔ ด
Thai name: dèk เด็ก child
End sound: t ต
Consonant class: Middle
Key: Unaspirated, **voiced**,
                 stop/tongue-teeth sound

Improve
If you use the English sound as in the word **d**o, there will be no problem. This **d** ด-sound is pronounced unaspirated as in English. There is no puff of air when the letter **d** is pronounced. Note that the Thai dɔɔ ด-sound is perhaps pronounced softer than the English **d**-sound, meaning that the vocal folds are vibrating somewhat less.

Most English speakers would not experience any difficulty with this sound.

Stop teeth sounds t ต, d ด   71

Description

This **d** ด-sound is a voiced and unaspirated glottal stop sound. The voiced sound means that the vocal folds are vibrating when the sound is produced. The place of articulation is alveolar, meaning that the front of the tongue is placed behind upper teeth against the front part of the alveolar ridge. The air flow is first stopped and then released with a plosive and vocal folds vibrating.

Similar English sounds for dɔɔ ด: **d**o, o**dd**, **d**ate
Rating: Good

Different ways to transliterate dɔɔ ด
Royal Thai: d
Other transliterations: d is used by most of the transliteration systems

Summary
Initial sound: dɔɔ ด
End sound: t ต
Consonant class: Middle
Manner of articulation: Unaspirated, voiced, stop/tongue consonant sound
Place of articulation: Teeth (Alveolar)

tɔɔ ด
Thai name: tàu เต่า turtle
End sound: t ต
Consonant class: Middle
Key: Unaspirated, **unvoiced**, glottal stop/tongue-teeth sound

Improve

This sound t ต-sound is again a bit tricky for English speakers, because in English, the letter **t** is pronounced aspirated at the beginning of words, as in word **tender** or **time**. However, this Thai sound is unaspirated and unvoiced. Most importantly therefore, make sure that there is no puff of air when you make this sound.

First, stop the airflow in the glottis and put the blade of you tongue behind the upper teeth, touching the alveolar ridge and then release the sound with a plosive. We transliterate this sound with **t**. The letter **t** stresses the fact that the sound is unaspirated. The tongue is resting against upper teeth towards alveolar ridge, and the sound is made with the blade of the tongue. The English sound is more likely to be made with the tip of the tongue rather than with the blade of the tongue and without the glottal stop. If you make the sound as in the English word **stop**, you are on the way.

Description

This **t** ต-sound is an unvoiced and unaspirated glottal stop teeth sound. The place of articulation is alveolar, meaning that the blade of the tongue is placed behind the upper teeth touching the front part of the alveolar ridge. The air flow is first stopped in the glottis and then released with a plosive.

Note Sometimes this sound is transliterated as **dt** with the remark that the Thai sound is between **d** and **t**. However, **d** is an unaspirated voiced consonant sound as in the English word **date**, and **t** is aspirated as in the English word **take**. This Thai **t** ต-sound is neither voiced nor aspirated. It is unvoiced and unaspirated. If you compare this sound with **d** ด-sound then the key is to make it **unvoiced**. If you compare it with **th** ท-sound, the key is to make it **unaspirated**. That way you should come to the same sound, **t** ต, which is an unaspirated glottal stop sound.

Put your hand in front of your mouth and feel when you practice making this sound. If there is still some puff of air coming, then the sound is not quite right. With a little practice you will get it right. Try first with **t** as in the English word **t**ender, and note there is a clear puff of air. Then learn to say the unaspirated **t** ต correctly.

English speakers often tend to hear the Thai sound **d** ต when, in fact, the **t** ต-sound is used. You need to train your ear in order to say and hear the correct sound. Use the sound files on the audio cd and/or a native Thai teacher to assist you with this sound. See more about how to make a glottal stop sound in the phonetic section, page 24.

Similar English sounds for tɔɔ ต: s**t**op, s**t**ep, s**t**rong
Rating: Not very good

Different ways to transliterate tɔɔ ต
Royal Thai: t
Other transliterations: t, dt

Summary
Initial sound: tɔɔ ต
End sound: t ต
Consonant class: Middle
Manner of articulation: Unaspirated, unvoiced, stop/tongue consonant sound
Place of articulation: Glottal stop/Teeth (Alveolar)

Note The sound **t** ต is pronounced unaspirated at both the beginning and end of a word or syllable.

2. Vowels

Half open central vowel sounds เออะ and เออ

	Front	Central	Back
Closed	ี อี, ii อี	ี อึ, ืื อือ	ู อุ, uu อู
Half open	e เอะ, ee เอ **เออะ,** **ออ เออ** o โอะ, oo โอ		
Open	ɛ แอะ, ɛɛ แอ	a อะ, aa อา	ɔ เอาะ, ɔɔ ออ

Improve
Please learn to separate this short เออะ-sound from its long counterpart ออ เออ.

Short เออะ-sound
If you use the English sound as in the word **a**bout or teach**er** for the short เออะ-sound, you are quite close. If you speak American English, please do not pronounce the **r**-sound like in the word teach**er**.

Long ออ เออ-sound
If you use the English sound as in the word h**er** for the long ออ เออ-sound, you are quite close. If you speak American English, please be aware that you should pronounce this long ออ เออ-sound without the **r**-sound. Ask your native teacher to help you get these sounds exactly right.

Description
These vowels are produced in the middle of the mouth, with the mouth half open. The lips are unrounded. Be aware that in Thai, the long and short vowels are pronounced the same. Only the duration is different. The

same does not apply in English. In English, the length of the vowel, often changes the quality of the sound.

Similar English sounds for short เออะ: **a**bout, teach**er**, **A**nglia
Rating: Quite good
Similar English sounds for long เออ: h**er**, b**ir**d, b**ur**n
Rating: Quite good

Different ways to transliterate
Short เออะ
Royal Thai: oe
Other transliterations: ə, oe, er, oe!, euh

Long เออ
Royal Thai: oe
Other transliterations: əə, oe, oe:, oeoe, eo, euh

Summary
Vowel length: Short เออะ and long เออ
Manner of articulation: Half open, unrounded vowel sounds
Place of articulation: Central

B. Sound exercise 6

(bɛ̀ɛp fɯ̀k-hàt thîi hòk แบบ ฝึก หัด ที่ หก)

d ด dɔɔ
t ต tɔɔ

เออะ, เออ

Examples (tuua-yàang ตัว อย่าง)
dên   เดิ้น   smart (slang)
dəən   เดิน   to walk

tə̀   เตอะ   (only a sound, no meaning)
təəm   เติม   to fill, to add

Repeating sounds learned so far (phûut sám พูด ซ้ำ)

din	ดิน	earth
tiin	ตีน	foot (not polite)
dù	ดุ	to scold
duu	ดู	to look, to see
tên	เต้น	to dance
thêet	เทศน์	sermon
bə̀ng	เบิ่ง	to look (Isaan dialect)
pə̀ət	เปิด	to open

Common expressions (kham thîi tʃái bɔ̀i-bɔ̀i คำ ที่ใช้ บ่อยๆ)

mâi-pen-rai	ไม่ เป็น ไร	Never mind. You are welcome.
mâi mii panhǎa	ไม่ มี ปัญหา	There is no problem.
mâi mii àrai	ไม่ มี อะไร	Nothing. There is nothing.
àrai-kɔ̂ɔ-dâai	อะไร ก็ได้	Anything is ok.

C. Practical learning tips

English speakers need to pay attention to the fact that the initial sounds in Thai can be **aspirated** such as **th** ท or **unaspirated** such as **t** ต. The end sounds in Thai are never aspirated. They are not released but kind of "buried" in the mouth.

When the initial sound is unaspirated in English, it tends to be voiced such as **b** in the word **be** or **k** in the word **go**. Therefore the initial sounds in English are usually divided into **aspirated** and **voiced** sounds. Voiced sounds are not usually aspirated either in English or in Thai.

Where possible, we give an English word with a similar sound for each Thai sound. When learning Thai you need to learn a new way of thinking as far as sounds and spelling are concerned. In English, the same letter can be pronounced one way in one word and another way in another word. This applies to vowel sounds in particular. The pronunciation in Thai is more consistent.

D. Reading exercise 6

Answers from the reading exercise 5 page 68
pɤ̀k   ปึก   massive, firm
thùuk   ถูก   cheap, right

Consonant class: Middle and high
End sound: Closed
Vowel length: Short and long
Tone: Low

Tone rule for the low tone
When a word starts with a **middle** or **high** class consonant, and when the final sound is **closed**, the tone is **low**.

Note that the **closed** end sound is sometimes also called a "stop end sound" or "dead ending".

See more about end sounds in Secret number 19 and about tone rules in the 20th Secret.

pɤ̀k ปึก
The word starts with the **middle** class consonant **p** ป, which is pronounced unaspirated as in the English word spend. There is no puff of air when the sound is produced. The short ɤ อึ-sound as in the English word sh**ou**ld (not an exact match) is written above the consonant **p** ป. The word ends with the **middle** class stop consonant **k** ก. All stop consonants make a **closed** final sound when situated at the end of a word or syllable.

Tone

The tone is **low**, since the word starts with a **middle** class consonant, and the end sound is closed.

The vowel sound can be either **short** or **long**.

Note You need to make sure that you know how to pronounce the vowel อึ อื correctly. Please see more about this in the 3rd Secret. Note also that the **k** ก-sound at the end is not released. It is a closed stop sound without aspiration.

thùuk ถูก

The word starts with the **high** class consonant **th** ถ, which is pronounced aspirated as in the English word **t**ime. There is a clear puff of air when the sound is produced. The long **uu** ู-sound as in the English word s**oo**n is written beneath the consonant **th** ถ. The word ends with the **middle** class stop consonant **k** ก. All stop consonants make a **closed** final sound when situated at the end of a word or syllable.

Tone

The tone is **low**, since the word starts with a **high** class consonant, and the end sound is **closed**.

The vowel sound can be either **short** or **long**.

Note that the **k** ก-sound at the end is not released. It is a closed stop sound without aspiration. Also note that there are only three different **closed** final sounds that appear at the end of a word or syllable.

They are **p** ป, **t** ต and **k** ก.

Middle and **high** class consonants with a **closed** ending can only constitute a **low** tone when there is no tone mark. The vowel sound can be either **short** or **long**.

Reading exercise

Try to figure out how the following words are pronounced in Thai:

พูด

เทพ

The correct transliterations are given in the next Secret, page 86.

Secret 7

Be aware that learning the Thai script does not help you to understand Thai sounds any better. Sounds are sounds, and it does not matter how they are written. You need to learn every sound first, one by one, and then how each is written in Thai.

Learning the Thai script, however, does help you to understand the Thai language in a far more profound way than if you are just relying on transliterations, which are written in many different ways.

Note If you are trying to learn Thai sounds from the Thai script, your task will be more difficult than learning all the sounds first. You may get confused and give up. So, learn all the sounds first and then subsequently the Thai script. There are many more alphabet symbols than actual sounds in the Thai language.

For example:
Let's suppose that you would like to know how the following symbols are pronounced:

ถ, ฐ, ท, ธ, ฑ, ฒ

You might spend a lot of time working out the exact pronunciation of each symbol. However, if you already know the sound is **th** as in the English word **t**ime, then you only need to memorize that all these consonants represent this sound, **th**.

The next group of sounds consists of fricative teeth sounds **s** ซ and **s** ส. Their end sound is **t** ต.

A. New sounds

I. Consonants

Fricative teeth sounds sɔɔ ซ and sɔ̌ɔ ส
Phonetically, these consonant sounds are called unvoiced, unaspirated alveolar fricative sounds. We call these sounds simply "fricative teeth sounds", since they are made by putting the blade of the tongue behind the front teeth against the alveolar ridge. The air is not stopped but directed through a narrow channel. The turbulent airflow makes a **friction**. Both sounds are made in the same way. The only difference is that the sɔɔ ซ-sound belongs to the low class consonant group and the sɔ̌ɔ ส-sound to the high class. Hence, they produce a different tone.

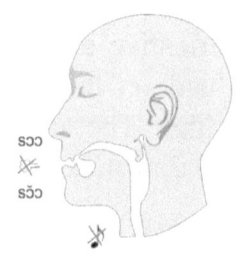

sɔɔ ซ
Thai name: sôo โซ่ chain
End sound: t ต
Consonant class: Low

sɔ̌ɔ ส
Thai name: sʉ̌ʉa เสือ tiger
End sound: t ต
Consonant class: High

Key: Unaspirated, unvoiced, **fricative**/tongue-teeth sounds

Improve
This sɔɔ ซ-sound is made similarly to the sound in the English word say. If you use the English way, there should be no problems. The English sound is sharper and is made more with the tip of the tongue while the Thai sound is made rather with the blade of the tongue.

The **sɔɔ** ซ-sound is made with the normal tone. The **sɔ̌ɔ** ส-sound is made in exactly the same way as the **sɔɔ** ซ-sound, but with a rising tone.

Description
Fricative **sɔɔ** ซ and **sɔ̌ɔ** ส-sounds are produced by placing the blade of the tongue behind the upper teeth touching the alveolar ridge. The air is forced through a narrow channel. The turbulent airflow makes a **friction**.

Note Some speakers may produce this sound by placing the tip of the tongue behind the lower teeth and then placing the blade of the tongue behind upper teeth touching the alveolar ridge. The sound is very similar, but perhaps in this case a bit softer.

Similar English sounds for **sɔɔ** ซ and **sɔ̌ɔ** ส: **s**ay, **c**ity, pa**ss**
Rating: Good

Different ways to transliterate **sɔɔ** ซ and **sɔ̌ɔ** ส
Royal Thai: s
Other transliterations: s is used by most of the transliteration systems

Summary
Initial sound: **sɔɔ** ซ and **sɔ̌ɔ** ส
End sound: t ต
Consonant class: Low and high
Manner of articulation: Unaspirated, unvoiced fricative/tongue consonant sound
Place of articulation: Teeth (Alveolar)

Note Please note that the end sound is the same while the initial sound changes. t ต is pronounced unaspirated at the end of a word or syllable. You must get used to the fact that in Thai, consonants are pronounced differently depending on whether they appear at the start or the end of a word or syllable. In English there is a voiced counterpart of this sound as **z** in the word **zone**. In Thai the voiced counterpart does not exist.

2. Vowels

Half open back vowel sounds ò โอะ and oo โอ

	Front	Central	Back
Closed	ì อิ, ii อี	ù อึ, uu อือ	ù อุ, uu อู
Half open	è เอะ, ee เอ	è เออะ, əə เออ	ò โอะ, oo โอ
Open	è แอะ, εε แอ	à อะ, aa อา	ò เอาะ, ɔɔ ออ

Improve

Learn to separate the short **ò** โอะ-sound from its long counterpart **oo** โอ.

Short **ò** โอะ-sound

This sound does not exist in its pure form in Standard English. When you say the word **folk**, you need to learn to say the short **ò** โอะ without the **ù** อุ-sound. Please make sure that you only use a pure short **ò** โอะ-sound, and do not make it into a vowel combination like **ou**. British people tend to make this short **ò** โอะ- sound into a schwa and say **ǝu**. However, American English users make a more clear **ou**-sound. Canadians and Scottish come closest to the correct sound. They seem to pronounce the word **folk** with a short **ò** โอะ-sound like in Thai.

> **Note** The short **ò** โอะ-sound does not appear very often in written Thai, since the convention is to omit the written vowel between two consonants but make the sound anyway. Despite this the short **ò** โอะ-sound is frequently used in Thai.

Long oo โอ-sound

Make this long oo โอ-sound longer than the short ò โอะ. It is close to the long ɔɔ ออ-sound as in the English word **law**. This English sound is a bit more open however. American English pronunciation is quite close if you say the word **go** long as **go**ou without the ù อุ-sound at the end. It seems that Australians produce this oo โอ-sound in the English word **law** quite close to how it is used in Thai. British and Americans tend to pronounce the word **law** a bit more open.

Description

These two vowel sounds are produced with the mouth half open. In other words, the tongue is not very close to the roof of the mouth when the sound is made. The place of articulation is at the back of the mouth, and lips are rounded.

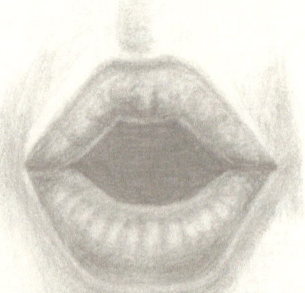

Note Be aware that in Thai, the long and short vowels are pronounced the same, only the duration is different. These two sounds in English are usually turned into a vowel combination such as **ou** or **əu**.

Please make sure that you are able to understand and produce these sounds correctly. You need to learn to make these sounds, short and long, without the **u**-sound at the end.

Similar English sounds for short ò โอะ: f**o**lk, r**o**ll, b**o**lt
Rating: Not very good
Similar English sounds for long oo โอ: g**o**, hell**o**, l**aw**
Rating: Not very good

Different ways to transliterate
Short ò โอะ
Royal Thai: o
Other transliterations: o, o!, ŏ, oh

Long oo โอ
Royal Thai: o
Other transliterations: oo, o, o:, oh

Summary
Vowel length: Short ò โอะ and long oo โอ
Manner of articulation: Half open, rounded vowel sounds
Place of articulation: Back

B. Sound exercise 7

(bɛ̀ɛp fɨ̀k-hàt thîi tsèt แบบ ฝึก หัด ที่ เจ็ด)

s ซ sɔɔ
s ส sɔ̆ɔ

ò โอะ, oo โอ

Examples (tuua-yàang ตัว อย่าง)
son	ซน	to be naughty
soon	โซน	zone, area
sòt	สด	fresh
sòot	โสด	single, unmarried

Repeating sounds learned so far (phûut sám พูด ซ้ำ)
sì	สิ	ending particle used to express emphasis
sǐi	สี	colour
tɨ̀k	ตึก	building
dɨ̀ɨm	ดื่ม	to drink
sùk	สุก	ripe
sǔun	ศูนย์	zero
tòt	ตด	to fart
dòot	โดด	to jump

Common expressions (kham thîi ʧái bɔ̀i-bɔ̀i คำ ที่ใช้ บ่อยๆ)

ʧâi	ใช่	Yes.
mâi-ʧâi	ไม่ ใช่	No.
ookee	โอเค	O.K.
mʉ̂ʉa-rài	เมื่อ ไหร่	When?

C. Practical learning tips

There are several ways to get practical help with Thai sounds. You can listen to audio material like cd's or read books with transliterations. There are also many websites, which give examples how to pronounce Thai sounds. You can also attend Thai classes.

One way is to get a private teacher. If you do this, it is better if you know exactly what kind of help you need before you engage the teacher. Do your homework first. In other words, you need to know your weak points and then ask the teacher to help and correct you. This book helps you on the way towards mastering Thai sounds and the writing system so that you can go on with your learning process. Use many teachers. There is no one right way. You need to find a way that works for you.

D. Reading exercise 7

Answers from the reading exercise 6 page 79

phûut	พูด	to speak
thêep	เทพ	God

Consonant class:	Low
End sound:	**Closed**
Vowel length:	Long
Tone:	Falling

Note that only a **low** class consonant can constitute the **falling** tone when there is no tone mark.

Tone rule for the falling tone
When a word or syllable starts with a **low** class consonant, ends with a **closed** final sound, and the vowel is **long**, the tone is **falling**.

phûut พูด
The word starts with the **low** class consonant **ph** พ which is pronounced aspirated as in the English word **p**aint. There is a clear puff of air when this sound is produced. The long **uu** ู-sound, as in the English word s**oo**n, is written under the low class consonant **ph** พ, and the long vowel sound comes after it. The word ends with the **middle** class stop consonant **d** ด, which is transliterated as an unaspirated stop sound **t** ด and constitutes an unaspirated **closed** final sound.

Tone
The tone is **falling**, since the word starts with a **low** class consonant and ends with a **closed** final sound, and the vowel is **long**.

If the vowel were short, the tone would be high.

Note The end sound is written as **d** ด but pronounced as **t** ด which is an unvoiced and unaspirated stop sound. Make sure that the **t** ด-sound at the end is not released. It is a stop sound without aspiration.

See more about end sounds (open and closed) in Secret number 19 and about tone rules in the 20th Secret.

thêep เทพ
The word starts with the **low** class consonant **th** ท which is pronounced strongly aspirated, even more than in the English word **t**ake. There is a clear puff of air when the sound is produced. The long vowel sound **ee** เ as in the English word p**ai**nt without the **i**-sound (not a very good match) is written before the letter **th** ท. Note however, that the long vowel sound comes after the consonant

th ท. The word ends with the **low** class stop sound **ph** พ, which is transliterated as an unaspirated **p** ป-sound. It constitutes an unaspirated **closed** final sound.

Tone
The tone is **falling** here, since the word starts with a **low** class consonant and ends with a **closed** end sound. The vowel is **long**.

If the vowel were short, the tone would be high.

Note that the end sound is written as **ph** พ but pronounced as **p** ป. Please make sure that the **p** ป-sound at the end is not released. It is a stop sound without aspiration and constitutes a **closed** final sound.

See more about end sounds (open and closed) in Secret number 19 and about tone rules in the 20th Secret.

Reading exercise

Try to figure out how the following words are pronounced in Thai:

ทุก

ซิป

The correct transliterations are given in the next Secret, page 99.

ॐ

Secret 8

Thai has two affricate sounds ʧ *as in the word* ʧɔ̂ɔp ชอบ *and* ts *as in the word* tsing จริง. *The first sound is* **aspirated** *and the second is* **unaspirated**. *English also has two affricate sounds* ʧ *as in the word* **child** *and* dʒ *as in the* **job**. *The first sound is* **aspirated**, *and the second is* **voiced**. *English stop sounds at the beginning of a word are divided into aspirated and voiced. In Thai, the similar initial sounds are aspirated and unaspirated.*

The next group of sounds is stop front sounds ʧ ช, ʧ ฉ and ts จ. The end sound for both is t ต.

Note that stop lip sounds constitute the end sound p บ, and stop teeth and front sounds produce t ต as the end sound.

A. New sounds

I. Consonants

Affricate front sounds ʧɔɔ ช, ʧɔ̌ɔ ฉ and tsɔɔ จ Phonetically, these consonant sounds are called alveolar-palatal affricates. Sometimes these sounds are also called post alveolar or even palatal stops. All this means that the tongue position may vary a bit. We call these consonants "stop front sounds" since the blade of the tongue is touching the roof in the front part of the mouth a bit further up from the alveolar ridge

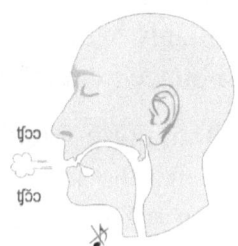

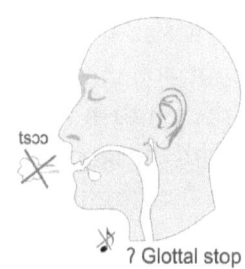

? Glottal stop

Stop front sounds ʧ ช, ʧ ฉ, ts จ

while these sounds are produced. These affricate sounds consist of two consonant sounds. One is a stop sound such as **t** and the other is a fricative sound such as **s** or ʃ. Affricates in Thai start with the stop sound **t**.

ʧɔɔ ช and ʧɔ̌ɔ ฉ are strongly aspirated while tsɔɔ จ is unaspirated.

ʧɔɔ ช
Thai name: ʧáang ช้าง elephant
End sound: t ด
Consonant class: **Low**

ʧɔ̌ɔ ฉ
Thai name: ʧhìng ฉิ่ง cymbals
End sound: t ด
Consonant class: **High**

Key: **Aspirated**, unvoiced, stop/tongue-front sound

Improve

If you use the English pronunciation as in the world **ch**ild, you are quite close. Note, however, that the English sound is produced mainly with the tip of the tongue, while the Thai sound is pronounced with the blade of the tongue.

Both these sounds are produced the same way. The only difference is that the ʧɔɔ ช-sound is pronounced with the normal tone and the ʧɔ̌ɔ ฉ-sound with the rising tone. Practice this in order to clarify the difference.

Practice it by putting your tongue behind the lower teeth and then put your lips as in the position for the long vowel sound **ii** อี as in the English word **eat**. Stop the airflow with the blade of the tongue with the stop sound **t** and then release it with the fricative sound ʃ as in the English word **sh**op.

Description

These two sounds are strongly aspirated, which means that a lot of air is released. In other words, there is a clear puff of air heard, similar to an **h**-sound, when the sound is made. The place of articulation is alveolo-palatal or post alveolar, meaning that the sound is articulated with the blade of the tongue further up behind the alveolar ridge. The term affricate is sometimes replaced with the term stop sound, which means that you first stop the air flow and then release it.

Note The only difference compared with the English sound as in the word **ch**ild is that the Thai sound is somewhat softer and is produced with the blade of the tongue instead of the tip of the tongue. ʧ denotes the fact that this sound is an aspirated stop sound. It also seems that English speakers tend to round their lips in order to increase the aspiration. In Thai, however, the lips are not rounded.

Similar English sounds for ʧɔɔ ช and ʧɔ̌ɔ ฉ: **ch**ild, tea**ch**, **ch**apter
Rating: Good

Different ways to transliterate ʧɔɔ ช and ʧɔ̌ɔ ฉ
Royal Thai: ch
Other transliterations: ʧ, ch, tsch, tsh, tɕʰ

Summary
Initial sound: ʧɔɔ ช and ʧɔ̌ɔ ฉ
End sound: t ด
Consonant class: Low and high
Manner of articulation: Aspirated, unvoiced, affricate/tongue consonant sound
Place of articulation: Front (Alveolar-palatal)

Note The most correct way to transliterate this sound is to use the international phonetic symbol tɕʰ. It is however not widely known and therefore seldom used.

The end sound **t** ต is pronounced unaspirated at the end of a word or syllable. You must get used to the fact that in Thai, consonants are pronounced differently depending on whether they appear at the start or the end of a word or syllable. However, the high class consonant ʧɔ̌ɔ ฉ does not appear as an end sound.

tsɔɔ จ ✂ ❀ ?
Thai name: tsaan จาน plate
Consonant class: Middle
End sound: **t** ต
Key: **Unaspirated**, unvoiced, **glottal stop**/
                   tongue-front sound

Improve

This **ts** จ-sound is produced the same way as **ʧ** ช. The only difference is that **ts** จ-sound is not aspirated. It is a glottal stop. The letter **j**, as in the English word **joy**, is often given as an example. This is, however, not quite right, since the English consonant **j** is voiced, but the Thai sound **ts** จ is unvoiced. We have given some sample words, but try to learn this sound without English examples. You need to learn a new sound. Get it right and you will be more easily understood by your Thai friends.

Practice it by putting your tongue behind the lower teeth and then put your lips in the position for the long vowel sound **ii** อี as in the English word **eat**. Stop the airflow first in the glottis and then make the sound with the blade of the tongue with the help of **t** and **s**.

Remember that not much air is released, meaning this sound is unaspirated. When the **s**-sound is made with the blade of the tongue and a bit deeper in the front of the mouth, it becomes softer than the English **s**-sound, which is usually clear and sharp. That way you come quite close to this sound **ts** จ.

Description

This sound is an unaspirated and unvoiced glottal stop sound, meaning there is no puff of air. The vocal folds are not vibrating when this sound is produced. The place of articulation is glottal stop/palatoalveolar or postalveolar, meaning that the sound is articulated in the glottis and made with the blade of the tongue behind the alveolar ridge.

Note This sound tsɔɔ จ is perhaps the most misunderstood Thai sound among non-native speakers. Therefore, we try to explain it here in detail.

The English j-sound as in the word John is a voiced palate-alveolar affricate and therefore not exactly the same as this Thai sound tsɔɔ จ. The term affricate is sometimes replaced with the term stop sound, which means that you first stop the air flow and then release it.

This Thai sound tsɔɔ จ is transliterated in many ways, examples include: **j, ch, c, dsch**. The most correct way to transliterate this sound would be to use the international phonetic symbol **tɕ**. It is not known very well however and therefore seldom used.

Note also that the Royal Thai uses **ch** for both the sounds ʧ ช and **ts** จ. This is perhaps because these two sounds are quite close to each other when spoken, and perhaps the aim has been to simplify the transliteration system. It is not correct, however, and can cause further misunderstanding.

Many transliteration systems use **ch** for ʧ ช and ʧ ฉ and **j** for **ts** จ. From that transliteration, it is not very easy to deduce that the only difference between these two sounds is that the first is an aspirated and the latter is an unaspirated. The English influence here is strong, and the sound **j** is often given as an example, which is then imitated by many other language groups and even by Thai teachers.

The good news is however that if you use **j** for this Thai sound tsɔɔ จ as in the English word **J**ohn, you are understood by Thais, since there is no other sound like that in Thai to confuse it with. Thai people hear what they are accustomed to hear instead of precisely what you say.

Similar English sounds for tsɔɔ จ: **g**in, **j**oy, **ts**unami
Rating: Not very good
Note that if you pronounce **ts**unami as it is written and not like **s**unami, you are close.

Different ways to transliterate **ts**ɔɔ จ
Royal Thai: ch
Other transliterations: ts, c, j, dsch, tɕ

Summary
Initial sound: tsɔɔ จ
End sound: t ต
Consonant class: Middle
Manner of articulation: Unaspirated, unvoiced, affricate/tongue consonant sound
Place of articulation: Glottal stop/front sound (Alveolar-palatal)

Note The end sound **t** ต is pronounced unaspirated at the end of a word or syllable. You must get used to the fact that in Thai, consonants are pronounced differently depending on whether they appear at the start or the end of a word or syllable.

2. Vowels

Open front vowels è แอะ and ɛɛ แอ

	Front	Central	Back
Closed	ì อิ, ii อี	ù อึ, uu อือ	ù อุ, uu อู
Half open	è เอะ, ee เอ	è เออะ, əə เออ	ò โอะ, oo โอ
Open	**è แอะ, ɛɛ แอ**	à อะ, aa อา	ò เอาะ, ɔɔ ออ

Improve
Learn to separate the short è แอะ-sound from its long counterpart ɛɛ แอ.

Short è แอะ-sound
If you use the English sound as in the word cat for the short è แอะ-sound, you are quite close.

Note that there is another English sound, which is a bit more closed, as in the word pet. It is somewhat similar but not exactly the same as the Thai sound è แอะ. Some English speakers tend to pronounce the short è แอะ-sound as in the English word hang longer than it is pronounced in Thai. Make sure that you always pronounce short vowel sounds short in Thai.

Long ɛɛ แอ-sound
The long ɛɛ แอ-sound is close to the English sound as in the word sad. If you use the English way you are quite close. Some English speakers tend to pronounce the long ɛɛ แอ as in the English word bad shorter than it is pronounced in Thai. Make sure that you always pronounce long vowel sounds long in Thai.

Ask a native Thai teacher to tell you if any improvement is needed and correct you as appropriate.

Open vowel sounds เอะ แอะ, แอ แอ

Description

These two vowel sounds are produced with the mouth open. In other words, the tongue is quite far from the roof of the mouth when you make these sounds. The place of articulation is at the front of the mouth and the lips are unrounded. Just be aware of the fact that in Thai, the long and short vowels are pronounced the same. Only the duration is different.

Make sure that you are able to understand and produce these sounds correctly. Ask your native teacher to help you get these sounds exactly right.

Note How to pronounce vowel sounds is not so important in English. Vowel sounds can often be dragged and drawled, and even changed a bit without losing the meaning. In Thai, you need to be much more exact in order to be understood. Note also that American English does not make any distinction, not even in phonetics, between short and long vowels. Don't mix up these two pairs of sounds, on the one hand the è เอะ and ee เอ and on the other hand è แอะ and εε แอ.

Similar English sounds for short è แอะ: **cat, hang, at**
Rating: Quite good, but pay close attention
Similar English sounds for long εε แอ: **sad, bad, mad**
Rating: Quite good, but pay close attention

Different ways to transliterate
Short è แอะ
Royal Thai: ae
Other transliterations: ε, ae, ae!, aĕ, air

Long εε แอ
Royal Thai: ae
Other transliterations: εε, ae, aeae, air, ae:

Summary
Vowel length: Short è แอะ and long ee เอ
Manner of articulation: Open, unrounded vowel sounds
Place of articulation: Front

B. Sound exercise 8

(bὲɛp fɯ̀k-hàt thîi pὲɛt แบบ ฝึก หัด ที่ แปด)

ʧ ช ʧɔɔ
ʧ ฉ ʧɔ̌ɔ
ts จ tsɔɔ

ɛ̀ แอะ, ɛɛ แอ

Examples (tuua-yàang ตัว อย่าง)
ʧɛ̀	แฉะ	wet
ʧɛ̌ɛ	แฉ	to reveal, to show
tsɛ̀	แจะ	only a sound, no meaning
tsɛ̀ɛk	แจก	to hand out

Repeating sounds learned so far (phûut sám พูด ซ้ำ)
sǐn	สิน	wealthy
sǐin	ศีล	religious rule
pìt	ปิด	to close
píip	ปี๊บ	bucket
phɯng	พึง	should
fɯ́ɯn	ฟื้น	to recover
tsùm	จุ่ม	to dip
tsùu	จู่	rush

Common expressions (kham thîi tʃái bòi-bòi คำ ที่ ใช้ บ่อยๆ)

khɔ̌ɔ-thôot
ขอ โทษ   Sorry! Excuse me!

àrai-ná
อะไร นะ   What? What did you say?

khun yàak dɯ̀ɯm àrai
คุณ อยาก ดื่ม อะไร   What would you like to drink?

tʃôok-dii-ná
โชค ดี นะ   Good luck! Cheers!

C. Practical learning tips

You need to learn a new, more consistent way of using letters and sounds similar to that which we use in this book. The English language does not give you much help in this regard. The English language is not consistent, and the same letter may denote many different sounds depending on the word it appears in.

For example, we have given here two words where the English letter **a** denotes two Thai sounds, **ɛ** แอะ as in the English word hang and **ɛɛ** แอ as in the English word sad.

However, the same letter is pronounced in English as **ei** in the word make, **ə** in about, **ɔɔ** together with **u** in taught and **aa** together with **u** in the word laugh and so on.

Build up your confidence gradually and start by using words which everyone uses daily. They are generally easily understood even if you do not pronounce the word exactly right. Learn to choose the right word for each situation. That is the Thai way.

D. Reading exercise 8

Answers from the reading exercise 7 page 88
thúk   ทุก   every, all
síp   ซิป   zipper

Consonant class: Low
End sound: **Closed**
Vowel length: Short
Tone: High

Only a **low** class consonant can constitute a **high** tone when there is no tone mark.

Tone rule 4 for the high tone
When a word or syllable starts with a **low** class consonant, ends with a **closed** final sound, and the vowel is **short**, then the tone is **high**.

thúk ทุก
The word starts with the **low** class consonant **th** ท, which is pronounced aspirated as in the English word **take**. There is a clear puff of air when this sound is produced. The short **ù** ุ-sound as in the English word **put** is written under the **low** class consonant **th** ท. The word ends with an unaspirated stop sound **k** ก, which makes a **closed** final sound.

Tone
The tone is **high**, since the word starts with a **low** class consonant, the vowel sound is **short**, and the end sound is **closed**.

If the vowel were **long**, then the tone would be **falling**.

Note The end sound is **k** ก, which is an unvoiced and unaspirated stop sound. Please make sure that the end sound is not released. It is a stop sound without aspiration.

síp ซิป

The word starts with the **low** class consonant **s** ซ, which is pronounced as in the English word **say**. The short vowel sound l อิ as in the English word **happy** is written above the **low** class consonant **s** ซ. The word ends with an unaspirated stop sound **p** ป, which makes a **closed** final sound.

Tone

The tone is **high**, since the word starts with a **low** class consonant, the vowel sound is **short**, and the end sound is **closed**.

If the vowel were **long**, then the tone would be **falling**.

Note Please make sure that the end sound **p** ป is not released. It is a stop sound without aspiration.

Reading exercise

Try to figure out how the following words are pronounced in Thai:

แจ

โสด

เทพ

ฤ

แฉ

The correct answers are given in the next Secret, page 109.

Secret 9

*It is very important to understand the Thai stop sounds. There are 6 unaspirated stop sounds (***k** ก, **ts** จ, **d** ด, **t** ต, **b** บ, **p** ป*) and 4 aspirated stops sounds (***kh** ค ข, **t͡ʃ** ช ฌ, **th** ท ฏ, **ph** พ ผ*) in Thai. In addition, there are 2 fricative sounds (***f** ฟ ฝ, **s** ช ส*), which function as stop sounds when at the end of a word. Many stop sounds are pronounced differently depending on whether they appear at the beginning or end of a word.*

End sounds:
p ป = **b** บ, **p** ป and **ph** พ ผ*
t ต = **t** ต, **d** ด, **ts** จ, **t͡ʃ** ช ฌ*, **th** ท ฏ, **f** ฟ ฝ* and **s** ช ส
k ก = **kh** ค ข, **k** ก
*   These Thai consonants do not appear as end sounds.

Note that when at the end of a word or syllable, all stop sounds are pronounced unaspirated without any puff of air.

The next group of sounds is **stop back sounds kh** ข, **kh** ค and **k** ก.

A. New sounds

I. Consonants

Stop back sounds khɔɔ ค, khɔ̌ɔ ข and kɔɔ ก Phonetically, these consonant sounds are called unvoiced velar stop sounds. We call them simply "stop back sounds", since they are made further back in the mouth, and the back of the tongue is touching the soft palate. The air is first stopped and then released with a plosive. khɔɔ ค and khɔ̌ɔ ข are strongly aspirated while kɔɔ ก is unaspirated.

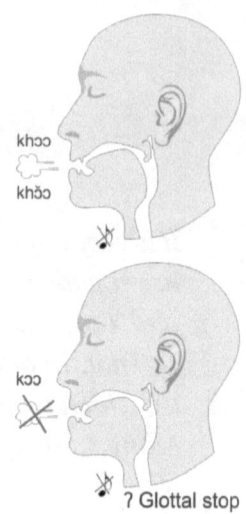

? Glottal stop

khɔɔ ค
Thai name: khwaai ควาย water buffalo
Consonant class: Low
End sound: k ก

khɔ̌ɔ ข
Thai name: khài ไข่ egg
Consonant class: High
End sound: k ก

Key: **Aspirated**, unvoiced, stop/tongue-back sound

Improve

The khɔɔ ค-sound is produced at the back of the mouth similar to the English sound as in the word **cat**. If you use the English way you will be quite close to the Thai sound. Please make this sound strongly aspirated; even more than in the English **kiss**. The khɔɔ ค-sound is pronounced with the normal tone.

The khɔ̌ɔ ข-sound is produced exactly the same way. The only difference is that it is pronounced with the rising tone.

Description

khɔɔ ค and khɔ̌ɔ ข-sounds are made further back in the mouth, and the back of the tongue is touching the soft palate. The air is first stopped and then released with a plosive. The place of articulation is velar, at the back part of the mouth. These sounds are aspirated, meaning that there is a clear puff of air when the sound is released.

Note The khɔɔ ค-sound belongs to the low class consonant group and khɔ̌ɔ ข belongs to the high class consonant group. They make a different tone when at the beginning of a word. Learn to pronounce khɔɔ ค with the **normal** tone and khɔ̌ɔ ข with the **rising** tone.

Similar English sounds for khɔɔ ค and khɔ̌ɔ: **c**at, **k**iss, **k**ettle
Rating: Good

Different ways to transliterate khɔɔ ค and khɔ̌ɔ
Royal Thai: kh
Other transliterations: kh, k

Summary
Initial sound: khɔɔ ค and khɔ̌ɔ
End sound: k ก
Consonant class: Low and high
Manner of articulation: Aspirated, unvoiced stop/tongue-consonant sounds
Place of articulation: Back (Velar)

Note The end sound k ก is pronounced unaspirated and unvoiced at the end of a word or syllable. You will get used to the fact that in Thai the end sound is pronounced differently to the initial sound.

kɔɔ ก
Thai name: kài ไก่ chicken
Consonant class: Middle
End sound: k ก
Key: **Unaspirated**, unvoiced, **glottal stop**/tongue-back sound

Improve

There is no English sound that is pronounced exactly as this Thai sound, kɔɔ ก, when it appears at the beginning of a word. It is produced unaspirated similar to the English sound as in the word **go** or **skin**. In English the letter **k** is pronounced unaspirated in the middle of a word. At the beginning of a word, the English letter **g** is also pronounced unaspirated but it is voiced. You should learn to produce an unvoiced **g** or an unaspirated **k** in order to come close to the Thai sound. The kɔɔ ก is pronounced with the normal tone.

Description

This sound is an unvoiced, unaspirated glottal stop consonant sound. The place of articulation is velar. Glottal stop consonant means that the air is first stopped in the glottis and then released with a plosive. Velar indicates the place of articulation, which is towards the back of the mouth.

Note If you pronounce **k** a little voiced as in the English word **go**, there is no possibility of misunderstanding, but if you pronounce it aspirated as in the English **k**, it may be confused with similar sounds, like **kh** ค or **kh** ข.

Note also that if **k** is pronounced unaspirated and **g** unvoiced, we come to the same sound. Make sure that there is no puff of air when you make this sound.

When you use in Thai the English **g** as in the word **go**, you should try to pronounce it unvoiced. However, the good news is that if you make this sound voiced as in the English word **go** you will be understood since there is no similar voiced Thai sound to be confused with it.

Similar English sounds for kɔɔ ก: **go, skin, skate**
Rating: Quite good, but pay attention

Different ways to transliterate kɔɔ ก
Royal Thai: k
Other transliterations: g, k

Summary
Initial sound: kɔɔ ก
End sound: k ก
Consonant class: Middle
Manner of articulation: Unaspirated, unvoiced, stop/tongue consonant sound
Place of articulation: Glottal stop/back sound (Velar)

Note The end sound **k** ก is pronounced unaspirated and unvoiced at the beginning and the end of a word or syllable. You must get used to the fact that in Thai, consonants are often pronounced differently depending on whether they appear at the start or the end of a word or syllable.

2. Vowels

Open central vowel sounds à อะ and aa อา

	Front	Central	Back
Closed	ì อิ, ii อี	ü อึ, ʉʉ อือ	ù อุ, uu อู
Half open	è เอะ, ee เอ	ə̀ เออะ, əə เออ	ò โอะ, oo โอ
Open	ɛ̀ แอะ, ɛɛ แอ	**à อะ, aa อา**	ɔ̀ เอาะ, ɔɔ ออ

Improve
Please learn to separate the short **à** อะ-sound from its long counterpart **aa** อา.

Short à อะ-sound
If you use the short **à** อะ-sound as in the English word **but**, you are quite close.

Long aa อา-sound
If you use the long **aa** อา-sound as in the English word **father**, you are quite close. The long English **aa** อา-sound may be, however, more at the back of the mouth while the Thai **aa** อา-sound is pronounced in the centre of the mouth.

Some English speakers, particularly Americans, tend to pronounce the long **aa** อา-sound similar to the sound in the English word **sad**, written phonetically as **sɛɛd**. They tend to say **pɛɛsport** instead of **paasport**. You need to be careful not to change the quality of the sound when you produce short and long vowels in Thai. Check this sound with your native Thai teacher so that you can pronounce it clearly and exactly right.

Description

When you produce this sound, the tongue is placed as far as possible from the roof of the mouth. The lips are unrounded and mouth open. The place of articulation is somewhere in the centre of the mouth.

Note In Thai, it is very important to maintain the correct length of a vowel. When the vowel length changes, the meaning of the word changes as well. The short and long vowels are pairs and are pronounced the same way. The only difference is the length of the vowel. In English, the place of articulation tends to change when the vowel length changes from short to long.

Similar English sounds for short **à** อะ: **but, run, flood**
Rating: Quite good
Similar English sounds for long **aa** อา: **father, vast, passport**
Rating: Quite good, but pay attention

Different ways to transliterate
Short à อะ
Royal Thai: a
Other transliterations: a, u, ah!, ǎ

Long aa อา
Royal Thai: a
Other transliterations: a, aa, ar, ah, a:

Summary
Vowel length: Short à อะ and long aa อา
Manner of articulation: Open unrounded vowel sounds
Place of articulation: Central

B. Sound exercise 9

(bɛ̀ɛp fɯ̀k-hàt thîi kâau แบบ ฝึก หัด ที่ เก้า)

kh ค khɔɔ
kh ข khɔ̌ɔ
k ก kɔɔ

à อะ, aa อา

Examples (tuua-yàang ตัว อย่าง)
khâ	ค่ะ	ending particle
khâa	ค่า	price
kàt	กัด	to bite
kàat	กาด	market (Northern dialect)

Repeating sounds learned so far (phûut sám พูด ซ้ำ)
khít	คิด	to think
khìit	ขีด	to mark
kɛ̀	แกะ	to unwrap
kɛ̀ɛ	แก่	to be old
tsɛ̀m	แจ่ม	bright
tsɛ̌ɛo	แจ๋ว	clear, excellent
khát	คัด	to select, to copy
khàat	ขาด	to be missing

Common expressions (kham thîi tʃái bɔ̀i-bɔ̀i คำ ที่ ใช้ บ่อยๆ)
duu-lɛɛ tuua-eeng ná	ดู แล ตัว เอง นะ	Take care of yourself.
khɔ̌ɔ hâi hǎai reu-reu	ขอ ให้ หาย เร็วๆ	Get well soon.
khít-thɯ̌ng mâak	คิด ถึง มาก	I miss you very much.
tsəə-kan ná khâ	เจอ กัน นะ ค่ะ	Let us meet soon.
tsəə-kan ná khráp	เจอ กัน นะ ครับ	Let us meet soon.

C. Practical learning tips

Be aware of the fact that we do not hear new sounds exactly as they are pronounced. We tend to hear them in the way we are accustomed to hear them in our own language. Therefore, it is not easy to learn new sounds just by listening.

You need to understand the new sounds in theory also, as explained in this book. Then practice and adjust your speaking until you can make new sounds correctly. By knowing how new sounds are made both in theory and practice, you will become more confident in learning Thai.

The Thai language is "feminine". That is to say it is spoken softly. Learn to use the sounds in a relaxed way. Small mistakes are easily forgiven, but too tense and serious an effort to try to speak this beautiful ancient language correctly may give you and even Thai people a headache!

D. Reading exercise 9

Answers from the reading exercise 8 page 100

tsɛɛ	แจ	close, nearby
sòot	โสด	single, unmarried
thêep	เทพ	God, divine being
thú	ทุ	bad, evil
tʃɛ̌ɛ	แฉ	to reveal, to show

Consonant class: Low, middle and high
End sound: **Open and closed**
Vowel length: Short and long
Tone: Normal, low, falling, high and rising
Here we have all five tones in the absence of a tone mark.

Open ending
Words with an **open** final sound without a tone mark can have **two** tones: **Normal** and **rising**.

Closed ending
Words with a **closed** final sound without a tone mark can have **three** tones: **Low**, **falling** and **high**.

Tone rule 1 for the normal tone
When a word starts with a **low** or **middle** class consonant, and when the word ends with an **open** final sound, the tone is **normal**.

tsɛɛ แจ
The word starts with **middle** class consonant **ts** จ, which is pronounced unaspirated similar to the English loan words pi**zz**a, **ts**unami or as in the word **J**ohn (not a very close match). This sound does not exist in its pure form in English. The long vowel sound **ɛɛ** แอ as in the English word s**a**d is written before the consonant **ts** จ. The vowel sound, however, comes after the consonant sound. The word ends with the long vowel sound **ɛɛ** แอ, which makes an **open** final sound.

Tone
The tone is **normal**, since the word starts with a **middle** class consonant and ends with an **open** sound.

If the final sound were closed, the tone would be low.

Note A **long** vowel sound at the end of a word makes an **open** final sound, and a **short** vowel sound makes a **closed** final sound.

Tone rule 2 for the low tone
When a word starts with a **middle** class or **high** class consonant, and when a word or syllable ends with a **closed** final sound, the tone is **low**.

sòot โสด
The word starts with the **high** class fricative consonant **s** ส. as in the English word **s**even. The long **oo** โอ-sound as in the English word g**o** without the u-sound (not a very close English match) is written before the high consonant **s** ส. The vowel sound comes after it, however. The word ends with the stop consonant sound **d** ด, which is pronounced at the end as an unaspirated **t** ต.

Tone
The tone is **low** in the first syllable, since the word starts with a **high** class consonant and ends with a **closed** final sound.

If the final sound were open, the tone would be rising.

Note This long **oo** โอ vowel sound does not exist in English in its pure form. Note also that the end sound is written as **d** ด but pronounced as **t** ต, which is an unvoiced and unaspirated stop sound. Make sure that the **t** ต-sound at the end is not released. It is a stop sound without aspiration.

Tone rule 3 for the falling tone
When a word or syllable starts with a **low** class consonant, ends with a **closed** final sound, and the vowel is **long**, the tone is **falling**.

thêep เทพ
The word starts with the **low** class consonant **th** ท, which is pronounced strongly aspirated; even more than in the English word **t**ake. There is a clear puff of air when the sound is produced. The long vowel sound **ee** เอ as in the English word p**ai**nt without the i-sound (not a very close match) is written before the letter **th** ท. Note that the vowel sound comes after the **th** ท-sound, however.

Tone
The tone is **falling** here, since the word starts with a **low** class consonant and ends with a **closed** final sound, and the vowel is **long**.

If the vowel were short, the tone would be high.

Note This long **ee** เอ vowel sound does not exist in English in its pure form. Note also that the end sound is written as **ph** พ but pronounced as **p** ป which is an unvoiced and unaspirated stop sound. Please make sure that the **p** ป-sound at the end is not released. It is a stop sound without aspiration.

Tone rule 4 for the high tone
When a word or syllable starts with a **low** class consonant, ends with a **closed final sound** and the vowel is **short**, the tone is **high**.

thú ทุ
The word starts with the **low** class consonant **th** ท, which is pronounced strongly aspirated; even more than in the English word take. There is a clear puff of air when the sound is produced. The short vowel sound **ù** ุ pronounced as in the English word look is written under the letter **th** ท. Note that the sound comes after the **th** ท-sound, however. The word ends with the short vowel sound **ù** ุ, which makes a **closed** final sound.

Tone
The tone is **high** here, since the word starts with a **low** class consonant and ends with a **closed** final sound, and the vowel is **short**.

If the vowel were long, the tone would be normal.

Note The word ends with a **short** vowel. It is a **stop** sound and constitutes a **closed** end sound. A **long** vowel sound at the end of a word makes an **open** final sound.

Tone rule 5 for the rising tone
When a word or syllable starts with a **high** class consonant, and ends with an **open** final sound, the tone is **rising**. The vowel can be either short or long.

ฉี๊ะ แฉ

The word starts with the high class consonant ฉ ฉ, which is pronounced strongly aspirated as in the English word **ch**ild. There is a clear puff of air when the sound is produced. The long vowel sound ɛɛ แอ is written before the consonant ฉ ฉ. However, the sound comes after it. The word ends with the long vowel sound ɛɛ แอ, which makes an **open** final sound.

Tone

The tone is **rising**, since the word starts with the **high** class consonant ฉ ฉ, and the end sound, the long ɛɛ แอ vowel sound, is **open**.

If the final sound were closed, the tone would be low.

Note In the absence of a tone mark, only a **high** class consonant can constitute the **rising** tone.

We have now studied all five tones: normal, low, falling, high and rising. See more about end sounds, open and closed, in Secret number 19 and about tone rules in the 20th Secret.

Reading exercise

Try to figure out how the following words are pronounced in Thai:

คือ

ถือ

ขีด

ซีด

คิด

The correct answers are given in the next Secret, page 120.

Secret 10

In Thai, there are only two types of glottal sounds: fricative glottal sounds and glottal stop sounds. The high class h ห *and low class* h ฮ *consonants are fricative glottal sounds. The glottal stop sound is often transliterated with the* ʔ *symbol. This symbol comes in front of the vowel sound when a word starts with a short or a long vowel sound.*

We have deliberately left out the glottal stop letter ʔ from the text in this book. It does not play a very important role as far as understanding vowel sounds are concerned. Phonetically, it would be more correct to use this letter, glottal stop ʔ.

However, it looks a bit awkward to write the word àang อ่าง like ʔàang อ่าง or àrai อะไร like ʔàrai อะไร. Hence the decision to leave it out. Moreover, in casual speech the glottal stop is not usually pronounced before the vowels.

A few transliteration systems use this letter ʔ, which looks a bit like a question mark. It can make some transliterations more confusing and difficult to understand.

However, it is very important to understand how the glottal stop is made as far as unaspirated stop consonants are concerned. See more about glottal stop in the phonetic section, page 26.

A. New sounds

I. Consonants

Fricative glottal sounds hɔɔ ฮ and hɔ̌ɔ ห
Phonetically, these sounds are called unvoiced, aspirated glottal fricative sounds. We call them simply "fricative glottal sounds", since they are made deeper in the mouth, in the glottal. The air is released through a narrow channel and is heavily aspirated. The turbulent airflow makes a **friction**.

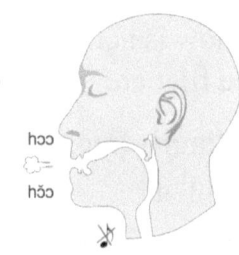

hɔɔ ฮ
Thai name: nók hûuk นกฮูก owl
End sound: Not applicable
Consonant class: Low

hɔ̌ɔ ห
Thai name: hìip หีบ chest
End sound: Not applicable
Consonant class: High

Key: **Aspirated**, unvoiced, glottal, fricative sounds

Improve
If you use the English sound as in the word **house**, there should not be any problems being understood. Please note that hɔɔ ฮ belongs to the low class consonant group. When it is at the beginning of a word or syllable, it produces a normal tone. Otherwise it is made exactly the same way as the high class consonant hɔ̌ɔ ห-sound, which is pronounced with the rising tone.

Description

These hɔɔ ฮ and hɔ̌ɔ ห-sounds are aspirated unvoiced fricative glottal sounds. The place of articulation is glottal, meaning the sound is produced deeper in the throat. Fricative sound means that the air flow is not stopped but directed through a narrow channel to make a friction.

Similar English sounds for hɔɔ ฮ and hɔ̌ɔ ห: **h**ave, **h**im, **h**ouse
Rating: Good

Different ways to transliterate hɔɔ ฮ and hɔ̌ɔ ห
Royal Thai: h
Other transliterations: h is used by most of the systems

Summary
Initial sound: hɔɔ ฮ and hɔ̌ɔ ห
Consonant class: Low and high
End sound: Not applicable
Manner of articulation: Aspirated, unvoiced, fricative consonant sounds
Place of articulation: Glottal

Note The glottal fricative consonants hɔɔ ฮ or hɔ̌ɔ ห do not appear as end sounds.

2. Vowels

Open back vowels ɔ̀ เอาะ and ɔɔ ออ

	Front	Central	Back
Closed	ì อิ, ii อี	ʉ̀ อึ, ʉʉ อือ	ù อุ, uu อู
Half open	è เอะ, ee เอ	ə̀ เออะ, əə เออ	ò โอะ, oo โอ
Open	ɛ̀ แอะ, ɛɛ แอ	à อะ, aa อา	**ɔ̀ เอาะ, ɔɔ ออ**

Improve

Please learn to distinguish the short ɔ̆ เอาะ-sound from its long counterpart ɔɔ ออ.

Short ɔ̆ เอาะ-sound

Standard English does not have the short ɔ̆ เอาะ-sound. Americans tend to pronounce this sound with lips unrounded. The British are closer, since they tend to pronounce this sound with lips rounded. Some Scottish and Australians seem to use this short ɔ̆ เอาะ-sound in words like n**o**t, g**o**t, s**o**ft.

One way to explain the short ɔ̆ เอาะ-sound is to use the long ɔɔ ออ-sound as in the word l**aw** but make it short. You may need help from a native teacher to get this sound right.

Long ɔɔ ออ-sound

If you make the long ɔɔ ออ-sound as in the English word l**aw**, you will be quite close. In Thai, this vowel is perhaps pronounced more open than the similar vowel in the English word.

Description

These two sounds are open, rounded back vowels. They are produced with the mouth open. In other words, the tongue is quite far away from the roof of the mouth when these sounds are made. The sounds are produced at the back of the mouth, and the lips are rounded.

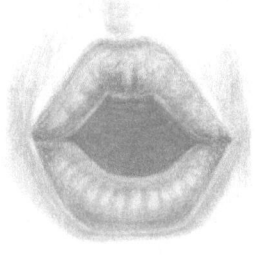

Similar English sounds for short ɔ̆ เอาะ: N**o**t, g**o**t, s**o**ft
Rating: Not very good
Similar English sounds for long ɔɔ ออ: **A**ll, c**au**ght, l**aw**
Rating: Quite good

Different ways to transliterate
Short ◌ॅ เอาะ
Royal Thai: o
Other transliterations: ɔ, aw, aw!

Long ɔɔ ออ
Royal Thai: o
Other transliterations: ɔɔ, ɔ:, o, oo, o:, aw, aw:, au

Note that the Royal Thai system also uses โ◌ โอะ for ◌ॅ เอาะ and ɔɔ ออ, and even for oo โอ, since it does not differentiate between long and short sounds, and merges these four sounds into a single symbol. This is not very helpful for your language studies!

You also need to learn to distinguish ◌ॅ เอาะ and ɔɔ ออ from โ◌ โอะ and oo โอ. Even though these sounds are quite close, you need to learn to hear, understand and reproduce the difference. The first sound is open and the second is half open. The good news is that if one uses a correct word in a given context, and manages to use the right tone, a slight pronunciation mistake is usually forgiven. Some foreign Thai teachers say that in practice and in everyday speech it does not matter whether you use the oo โอ-sound or ɔɔ ออ. However, native Thai teachers would disagree.

Summary
Length of the vowel: Short ◌ॅ เอาะ and long ɔɔ ออ
Manner of articulation: Rounded open vowel sounds
Place of articulation: Back

B. Sound exercise 10 🎧

(bèɛp fùk-hàt thîi sìp แบบ ฝึก หัด ที่ สิบ)

h ฮ hɔɔ
h ห hɔ̌ɔ

◌ॅ เอาะ, ɔɔ ออ

Examples (tuua-yàang ตัว อย่าง)

hɔ̂ng	ห้อง	room
hɔ̌ɔm	หอม	to smell
hɔ̂ng-gong	ฮ่องกง	Hong Kong
hɔ́ɔ	ฮ้อ	good (Chinese word)

Repeating sounds learned so far (phûut sám พูด ซ้ำ)

hèt	เห็ด	mushroom
hèet	เหตุ	reason
hɛ̀ng	แห่ง	place
hɛ̂ɛng	แห้ง	dry
bòt	บท	lesson
bòot	โบสถ์	church
tɔ̂ng	ต้อง	must
thɔ́ɔng	ท้อง	stomach

Common expressions (kham thîi tʃái bɔ̀i-bɔ̀i คำ ที่ใช้ บ่อยๆ)

khun tʃɯ̂ɯ àrai
คุณ ชื่อ อะไร   What is your name?

tsing-tsing
จริง จริง   Really!

maa nîi nɔ̀i khráp / khâ
มา นี่ หน่อย ครับ / ค่ะ   Please come here!

yàak khui kàp khun nɔ̀i
อยาก คุย กับ คุณ หน่อย   I would like to chat with you a little.

C. Practical learning tips

Be more concerned with 'how' rather than 'why'. For Thai people, language is a means for communication and having fun, not a complicated theory to be understood. Thai people say "right, but we do not say it like that". There is no why!

The Thai alphabetic order does not contain vowels, since a word can not start with a vowel in the Thai language. If there is a vowel sound at the beginning of a word, it always starts with the symbol -อ. Hence, all the words starting with a vowel sound are listed under this symbol -อ in the dictionary.

Example:
ìm	อิ่ม	to be full
eeng	เอง	oneself

In the Thai language vowels play a more important role than in English which depends more on consonants. Thai vowels are generally long unless marked short. Pronunciation of Thai vowels needs to be clear.

Thai vowels are not given names in the same way as consonants, since it is not easy to confuse one vowel with another if pronounced clearly. Every consonant is given a name linking it to a particular word in Thai because there are multiple consonants that produce the same sound.

D. Reading exercise 10

Answers from the reading exercise 9 page 113
khuu	คือ	to be, to mean, is
khìit	ขีด	to draw
ch̶ʉ̶ʉt	ซืด	tasteless

khít	คิด	to think
thʉ̌ʉ	ถือ	to hold, to carry

Consonant class: Low, middle and high
End sound: **Open and closed**
Vowel length: Long and short
Tone: Normal, low, falling, high and rising

Here we have all five tones in the absence of a tone mark.

Open ending
Words with an **open** ending without a tone mark can have **two** tones: **normal** and **rising**.

Closed ending
When the ending is **closed** without a tone mark, a word can have **three** tones: **low**, **falling** and **high**.

> **Note** See more about end sounds in Secret number 19.

Tone rule I for the normal tone
When a word starts with a **low** or **middle class** consonant, and when a word ends with an **open final sound**, the tone is **normal**.

khʉʉ คือ
The word starts with the **low** class consonant kh ค. The consonant kh ค as in the English word **cat** is pronounced strongly aspirated; even more than in English. There is a clear puff of air when the sound is produced. The long vowel ʉʉ อือ-sound as in the English word **rude** (not a close English match) is written above the consonant kh ค. The word ends with the long vowel ʉʉ อือ-sound, which makes an **open** final sound.

Tone
The tone is **normal**, since the word starts with a **low class** consonant, and the end sound is an **open**, long vowel sound.

The tone would be **high** if the vowel sound were **short**.

Note We need the symbol -อ at the end of the word kh**uu** คือ. If you are not sure about the **uu** อือ-sound, please go back to the 3rd Secret and review this sound once more.

Also be aware that a **long** vowel sound at the end of a word makes an **open** final sound, and a **short** vowel sound makes a **closed** final sound.

Tone rule 2 for the low tone

When a word or syllable starts with a **middle** class or a **high** class consonant, ends with a **closed** final sound, the tone is **low**. The vowel can be either short or long.

khìit ขีด

The word starts with the high class consonant **kh** ข, which is pronounced strongly aspirated; even more than in the English word **k**iss. There is a clear puff of air when the sound is produced. The long vowel sound **ii** อี as in the English word s**ee**, is written above the high class consonant **kh** ข. The word ends with the **middle** class stop consonant **d** ด, which is pronounced as an unaspirated **t** ต at the end of a word, and makes a **closed** final sound.

Tone

The tone is **low**, since the word starts with a **high class** consonant and the end sound is **closed**.

The tone would be **low** even if the vowel sound were **short**.

Note The end sound is written as **d** ด but pronounced as **t** ต, which is an unvoiced and unaspirated stop sound. Make sure that the **t** ต-sound at the end is not released. It is a stop sound without aspiration.

Tone rule 3 for the falling tone

When a word or syllable starts with a **low** class consonant, ends with a **closed** final sound, and the vowel is **long**, the tone is **falling**.

ฉืdt ซืด tasteless
The word starts with the **low** class consonant ฉ ช, which is pronounced strongly aspirated; even more than in the English word **ch**ild. There is a clear puff of air when the sound is produced. The long ืu อือ-sound (no close English match) is written above of the low class consonant ฉ ช. The word ends with the middle class stop consonant **d** ด, which is pronounced as an unaspirated **t** ด at the end, and makes a **closed** final sound.

Tone
The tone is **falling**, since the word starts with a **low** class consonant, the vowel sound is **long**, and the end sound is **closed**.

If the vowel were short, then the tone would be high.

Note When there is no tone mark, a **low** class consonant is the only consonant which can produce a **falling** tone or a **high** tone.

If you are not sure about the ืu อือ-sound, please go back to the 3rd Secret and review this sound once more.

Tone rule 4 for the high tone
When a word or syllable starts with a **low** class consonant, ends with a **closed** final sound, and the vowel is **short**, the tone is **high**.

khít คิด
The word starts with the **low** class consonant **kh** ค, which is pronounced strongly aspirated; even more than in the English word **k**ey. There is a clear puff of air when this sound is produced. The short vowel sound ิ อิ as in the English word happy is written above the low class consonant **kh** ค. The word ends with the middle class stop consonant **d** ด, which is pronounced as an unaspirated **t** ด at the end of a word and makes a **closed** final sound.

Tone
The tone is **high**, since the word starts with a **low** class consonant, the vowel is **short**, and the end sound is **closed**.

If the vowel were **long**, then the tone would be **falling**.

Note When there is no tone mark, only a **low** class consonant can produce a **high** or a **falling** tone.

Tone rule 5 for the rising tone
When a word or syllable starts with a **high class consonant** and ends with an **open** final sound, the tone is **rising**. The vowel can be either short or long.

th<s>ʉ</s> ถือ
The word starts with the **high** class consonant **th** ถ, which is pronounced strongly aspirated; even more than in the English word take. There is a clear puff of air when the sound is produced. The long <s>ʉʉ</s> อือ-sound (no close English match) is written above the **high** class consonant **th** ถ. The word ends with the long vowel <s>ʉʉ</s> อือ-sound, which constitutes an **open** final sound.

Tone
The tone is **rising**, since the word starts with a **high** class consonant, and the end sound is **open**.

Note When there is no tone mark, only a **high** class consonant can produce a **rising** tone.

If you are not sure about the <s>ʉʉ</s> อือ-sound, please go back to the 3rd Secret and review this sound once more.

See more about end sounds in Secret number 19, and about tone rules in the 20th Secret.

Reading exercise

Try to figure out how the following words are pronounced in Thai:

เฮฮา

เกาะ

โฮสต์

นะ

หอ

The correct transliterations are given in the next Secret, page 134.

Secret 11

*Sonorant sounds play a very important part in the Thai tonal system. All sonorant sounds belong to the low class consonant group. They are also called "**single sounds**" since they do not have any pair sound in the high class consonant group as stop and fricative sounds have. Sonorant sounds, long vowels and vowel combinations form so called "**open final sounds**" in the Thai tonal system.*

As the last group of sounds we look at all the sonorant consonant sounds. Sonorant consonant sounds are **m** ม, **n** น, **l** ล, **r** ร, **ng** ง, **y** ย and **w** ว.

Sonorant sounds are made in such a way that the air flow is not restricted. The final sound can be prolonged without any difficulty, the opposite to stop sounds where the sound is stopped. Sonorant sounds are "**open final sounds**" in the Thai tonal system.

All sonorant sounds are **voiced** and belong to the **low class** consonant group. In both Thai and English all sonorant sounds are **unaspirated**.

The end sounds for sonorant sounds are **n** น, **m** ม or **ng** ง. With the semi-vowels **y** ย and **w** ว the end sounds are **i** and **u** respectively.

Note A long vowel is also a sonorant sound at the end of a word.

A. New sounds

I. Consonants

Sonorant nasal sounds mɔɔ ม and nɔɔ น
Phonetically, these consonant sounds are called voiced, unaspirated, nasal sounds. We call them simply "nasal lip sounds" and "nasal teeth sounds", since they are produced by directing the air through the nose. mɔɔ ม is articulated by both lips, kept together, and nɔɔ น is articulated by putting the tongue behind the front teeth against the alveolar ridge.

mɔɔ ม ♪
Thai name: máa ม้า horse
Consonant class: Low
End sound: m ม
Key: Unaspirated, voiced, sonorant, **nasal/lip** sound

Improve
This consonant sound is made like in the English word **m**ilk. If you use the English way, there will be no problem.

Description
This mɔɔ ม-sound is a voiced unaspirated nasal sound, meaning that the vocal folds are vibrating, and the air is directed through the nose. The sound is bilabial, meaning that the place of articulation is the lips.

> **Note** In Thai as in English, there are three nasal sounds, **m** ม, **n** น and **ng** ง. They are each articulated in a different place in the mouth. In English, the **ng** ง-sound does not appear at the beginning of a word as it does in Thai.

Similar English sounds for มɔɔ ม: **m**eeting, **m**an, **m**ilk
Rating: Good

Different ways to transliterate มɔɔ ม
Royal Thai: m
Other transliterations: m is used by most of the systems

Summary
Initial sound: mɔɔ ม
End sound: m ม
Consonant class: Low
Manner of articulation: Unaspirated, voiced, sonorant nasal consonant sound
Place of articulation: Lips (Bilabial)

Note The end sound m ม is the same as the initial sound.

nɔɔ น
Thai name: nǔu หนู mouse
Consonant class: Low
End sound: n น
Key: Unaspirated, voiced, sonorant, **nasal**/**teeth** sound

Improve
The nɔɔ น-sound is quite close to the English sound, and there should be no problem if you use the English sound.

Description
This n น-sound is a voiced, unaspirated, nasal sound, meaning that the vocal folds are vibrating, and the air is directed through the nose. The tongue is placed behind the upper teeth towards the alveolar ridge.

Similar English sounds for nɔɔ น: **n**eat, **n**ice, **n**et
Rating: Good

Different ways to transliterate ก ว น
Royal Thai: n
Other transliterations: n is used by most of the systems

Summary
Initial sound: ก ว น
End sound: n น
Consonant class: Low
Manner of articulation: Unaspirated, voiced, sonorant nasal consonant sound
Place of articulation: Teeth (Alveolar)

Note The end sound for n น is the same as the initial sound.

2. Vowels

Special vowels au เอา and am อำ

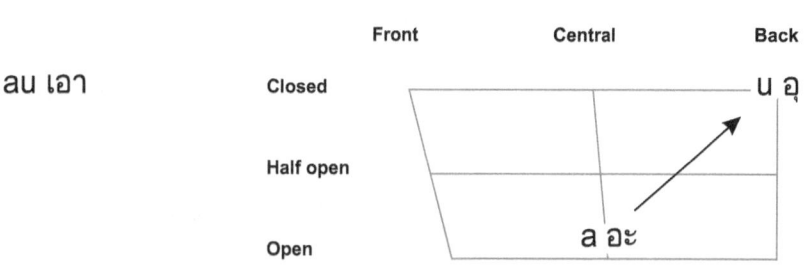

Improve

Please learn to separate the short **au** เอา-sound from the similar long sound **aau** อาว.

The long sound is given here just for comparison, and it is not listed in the Thai vowel list.

This short **au** เอา-sound starts with the short **a** อะ and ends with the short **ù** อุ-sound. If you make this sound like in the English word **now**, you will be quite close.

Description

This vowel combination consists of two sounds **à** อะ and **ù** อุ, but is written with the special symbol **au** เอา. It starts with the open unrounded vowel **à** อะ and ends with the closed **ù** อุ vowel sound.

Similar English sounds for au เอา: n**ow**, tr**ou**t, br**ow**n
Rating: Good

Different ways to transliterate au เอา
Royal Thai: au
Other transliterations: au, ao, aw

Summary
Vowel lenght: Short au เอา
Manner of articulation: From open unrounded **à** อะ-sound to closed rounded **ù** อุ-sound
Place of articulation: From central to back

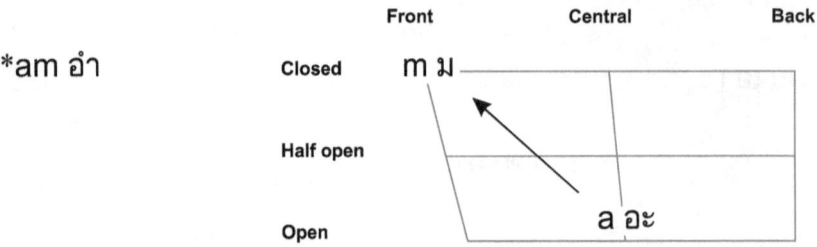

*am อำ

* Note the consonant **m** ม is not a vowel, but it is a part of this vowel combination. This sound **am** อำ is classified in Thai as a special vowel.

Please learn to separate the short **am** อำ-sound from the similar long sound **aam** อาม

The long sound is given here just for comparison, and it is not listed in the Thai vowel list.

This sound is made like in the English word s**o**m**e**. If you use the English way, you will be quite close.

Description
This vowel combination consists of two sounds **à** อะ and **m** ม, but is written with one special symbol, **am** อำ. It starts with the open unrounded short vowel **à** อะ and ends with the consonant sound **m** ม.

Similar English sounds for **am** อำ: **um**brella, s**om**e, h**um**ble
Rating: Good

Different ways to transliterate **am** อำ
Royal Thai: am
Other transliterations: am, um

Summary
Vowel length: Short am อำ
Manner of articulation: From open unrounded vowel à อะ-sound ending with the consonant sound **m** ม.
Place of articulation: From centre to a lip sound

Note These two sounds **au** เอา and **am** อำ belong to the group of so called special vowels in Thai. They may also be called vowel combinations or diphthongs. The sound **am** อำ is a very special case, since it is the only vowel sound that ends with a consonant. It is listed in the Thai vowel list, however.

B. Sound exercise 11

(bɛ̀ɛp fùk-hàt thîi sìp èt แบบ ฝึก หัด ที่ สิบ เอ็ด)

m ม mɔɔ
n น nɔɔ

au เอา,
aau อาว*

am อำ
aam อาม*

> * Please note that the long sound is given here just for comparison. Please see more about long vowel combinations in Secret 16.

Examples (tuua-yàang ตัว อย่าง)

mǎu	เหมา	to presume, to rent
nǎau	หนาว	cold
nam	นำ	to lead
naam	นาม	name

Repeating sounds learned so far (phûut sám พูด ซ้ำ)

sám	ซ้ำ	to repeat
sǎam	สาม	three
nâu	เน่า	rotten
nǎau	หนาว	cold
khâu	เข้า	to enter
khâau	ข้าว	rice
sǎu	เสา	pillar, post
sǎau	สาว	girl, young woman

Common expressions (kham thîi tʃái bɔ̀i-bɔ̀i คำ ที่ใช้ บ่อยๆ)

khun maa tʃàak nǎi	คุณ มา จาก ไหน	Where do you come from?
sĭang dang kəən-pai	เสียง ดัง เกิน ไป	It is too noisy here!
tɔ̂ng pai lɛ́ɛo	ต้อง ไป แล้ว	I need to go now.
thammai lâ	ทำไม ล่ะ	Why?

C. Practical learning tips

As a serious language student it makes sense to get a dictionary early on in your studies. There are basically two kinds:

The first includes transliteration and is meant for westerners. An example would be: Benjawan Poomsan Becker's *Thai-English, English-Thai Dictionary*. Note that Becker uses a somewhat different transliteration for some unaspirated consonant sounds (**t** and **p**) compared with this book. You might already be aware that almost every learning book in Thai uses it own transliteration system. Our advice would be, to first learn one system well, for instance the one in this book, then it will be much easier to adjust to other systems.

The second kind of dictionary is for native Thai students and westerners who are able to understand at least the basics of the Thai script. An example would be: Dr. Wit Thiengburanathum's *Thai-English Dictionary*. If you buy this second type of dictionary, make sure that there is a complete alphabetic list written on the outer margins of every page. This will help you to keep track of the alphabetic order, and makes it easier to find words.

It is somewhat harder to look up words in a Thai rather than an English dictionary, since there are many different consonants with sounds that are the same or close to each other. All vowels are listed under the symbol -อ. Many other initial consonant sounds are also listed under the silent high class consonant **h** ห, which functions as a tone regulator.

A dictionary can only be used as an aid to learning, and cannot be trusted when trying to find a suitable word for a specific situation. This is even more true in Thai than many other languages. It contains a large number of words, which are not used by ordinary Thais in everyday speech. On the other hand, it may not contain some newer words or slang words commonly used by Thai people.

It is better to learn Thai words from sentences spoken in real-life situations.

D. Reading exercise 11

Answers from the reading exercise 10 page 125

hee haa	เฮฮา	to revel, to enjoy oneself
kɔ̀	เกาะ	to cling, island
hóot	โฮสต์	host
ná	นะ	ending particle
hɔ̌ɔ	หอ	towel, hall

Consonant class: Low, middle and high
End sound: **Open and closed**
Vowel length: Short and long
Tone: Normal, low, falling, high and rising
Here we have all five tones in the absence of a tone mark.

Open ending
Words with an **open** ending without a tone mark can have **two** tones, **normal** and **rising**.

Closed ending
When the ending is **closed** without a tone mark, a word can have **three** tones, **low**, **falling** and **high**.

> Note   Please see more about end sounds in the 19th Secret.

Tone rule 1 for the normal tone
When a word or syllable starts with a **low** or **middle** class consonant, and when the word ends with an **open** final sound, the tone is **normal**.

hee haa เฮฮา
The word starts with the **low** class consonant **h** ฮ, which is pronounced aspirated as in the English word hence. The long **ee** เอ

vowel sound as in the English word s**ai**l without the **i**-sound (not a very close match) is written before the low class consonant **h** ฮ, but the vowel sound comes after the consonant sound. The long **aa** อา-sound as in the English word f**a**ther is written after the second high class consonant **h** ห.

Both syllables end with a long vowel sound, the first one with the long **ee** เอ and the second one with long **aa** อา, these make an **open** final sound.

Tone
The tone here is **normal** in the first and second syllable since they both start with a low class consonant, and the end sounds are **open**.

If the final sound were closed, the tone would be **falling**.

Note The other vowel sound **ee** เอ is written before the consonant and the other **aa** อา after the consonant. In both cases the vowel sound comes after the consonant **h** ฮ.

Tone rule 2 for the low tone
When a word or syllable starts with a **middle** class or **high** class consonant, ends with a **closed** final sound, the tone is **low**.

k**ɔ̀** เกาะ
The word starts with the **middle** class consonant **k** ก as in the English word **sk**in. The consonant **k** ก is pronounced unaspirated. There is no puff of air when the sound is produced. The short vowel sound **ɔ** เอาะ as in the English word n**o**t (not a very close match) is written before and after the consonant. The end sound is **closed**, since the word ends with the short vowel sound, **ɔ** เอาะ.

Tone
The tone is **low**, since the word starts with a **middle** class consonant, and the end sound is **closed**.

If the vowel sound were long, the tone would be **normal**.

Note Make sure that you pronounce the consonant **k** ก unvoiced and unaspirated at the beginning of a word or syllable. Note also that the short vowel ɔ̀ เอาะ is written quite differently from its long counterpart ɔɔ ออ.

Tone rule 3 for the low tone
When a word or syllable starts with a **low** class consonant, ends with a **closed** final sound, and when the vowel is **long**, the tone is **low**.

hôot โฮสต์
The word starts with the **low** class consonant **h** ฮ, which is pronounced aspirated as in the English word **h**ence. There is a clear puff of air when the sound is produced. The long vowel sound **oo** โอ as in the English word g**o** without the **u**-sound (not a very close match) is written before the low class consonant **h** ฮ. Note that the long vowel sound **oo** โอ comes after the consonant, however. The word ends with the **high** class fricative consonant **s** ส, which is pronounced at the end as **t** ต. The stop consonant **t** ต makes a **closed** end sound.

Tone
The tone should be **falling**, since the word starts with a **low** class consonant, the vowel is **long**, and the end sound is **closed**. However, it is high. Often foreign English words are pronounced with the high tone even though the tone rule suggest different tone.

If the vowel sound were **short**, the tone would be **high**.

Note There is a special symbol **kaaran** การันต์ above the letter **t** ต. **Kaaran** implies that the sound is silent and is not pronounced. This symbol is usually used with foreign words, which have been adapted to Thai.

Tone rule 4 for the high tone
When a word or syllable starts with a **low** class consonant, ends with a **closed** final sound, and the vowel is **short**, the tone is **high**.

ná นะ
The word starts with the **low** class nasal sonorant consonant **n** น as in the English word **n**ame. The short vowel sound **à** อะ as in the English word b**u**t is written after the low class consonant **n** น. The end sound is **closed**, since the word ends with the short vowel sound, **à** อะ.

Tone
The tone is **high**, since the word starts with a **low** class consonant, the vowel is short and the end sound is **closed**.

The short vowel always produces a closed end sound.

If the vowel sound were **long**, the tone would be **normal**.

Note A **short** vowel is regarded as a stop sound and constitutes a **closed** final sound. Also, when the short **à** อะ-sound is written at the end of a word, it is simply marked as ะ.

Tone rule 5 for the rising tone
When a word or syllable starts with a **high** class consonant and ends with an **open** final sound, the tone is **rising**. The vowel can be either short or long.

hɔ̌ɔ หอ
The word starts with the **high** class consonant **h** ห, which is pronounced aspirated as in the English word **h**er. There is a clear puff of air when the sound is produced. The long vowel sound ɔɔ ออ as in the English word **law** is written after the high class consonant **h** ห. The word ends with the long vowel ɔɔ ออ, which makes an **open** final sound.

Tone

The tone is **rising**, since the word starts with a **high** class consonant, and the end sound is **open**.

If the final sound were **closed**, the tone would be **low**.

Note The **high** class consonants are able to make a **rising** tone when the final sound is open. The **low** and **middle** class consonants make a **normal** tone when the final sound is open.

Reading exercise

Try to figure out how the following words are pronounced in Thai:

เน่า

แม่น

เก่า

ดำ

เผ่า

The correct answers are given in the next Secret, page 146.

∽

Secret 12

In Thai the ร -letter and sound has a number of unique features that can sometimes cause confusion. Understanding these will be an important part of your learning. Whenever you see the written ร -letter in a word at the end or between two consonants, you will need to know the rules for how to pronounce it. In addition, the consonant ร can turn itself into a vowel in some cases. Furthermore, many Thai people like to replace the ร-sound in spoken Thai with the plain ล-sound, mainly perhaps because it is easier to pronounce. In this case you will need to figure out the meaning from the context.

See more about rules for how to pronounce the written consonant ร in the 21st Secret.

A. New sounds

I. Consonants

Sonorant teeth sounds rɔɔ ร and lɔɔ ล
Phonetically, the rɔɔ ร-sound is called a voiced alveolar trill, while the lɔɔ ล-sound is called a voiced alveolar lateral. We call these sounds "teeth trills" and "teeth laterals". They are made by putting the tongue behind the front teeth against the alveolar ridge.

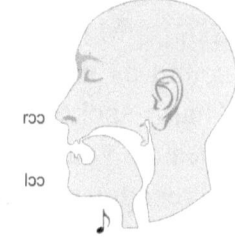

We take these two consonant sounds together, since many Thais do not pronounce the รoo ร-sound properly or replace it with the loo ล-sound. English speakers can experience some difficulties making the correct Thai รoo ร-sound as well.

Note also that both of these sounds always constitute n น as the end sound.

รoo ร ♪
Thai name: ruua เรือ boat
Consonant class: Low
End sound: n น
Key: Unaspirated, voiced, sonorant, **trill/teeth** sound

Improve
If you use the English sound as in the word **red**, you are on the way. The Thai sound may be a little difficult for English speakers, since it is pronounced a bit differently in Thai. The English sound is much "looser" and is made deeper in the mouth. Learn to roll the รoo ร-sound in Thai. If you know the Spanish **r**, then try to imitate that.

Description
This sound is a voiced trill. The place of articulation is alveolar. That means that you need to place the tongue behind the upper front teeth against the alveolar ridge when you produce the รoo ร-sound.

Note Many Thai speakers substitute this **r** ร-sound with the **l** ล-sound as in the English world like. So, it is quite common that Thai is spoken without the correct Thai **r** ร-sound. As a non-native speaker, you should use the correct sound. You will, however, need to recognise when Thai people replace **r** ร with **l** ล. That can be tricky, at least at the beginning.

Standard Thai (TV, educated people etc.), Southern dialect and Thais of Cambodian origin all tend to use the correct r ร-sound. All schoolchildren are taught to speak Standard Thai, but at home and elsewhere outside school they usually replace the r ร-sound with the l ล-sound. The cultural pressure in everyday speech is strong. Even educated people often use the l ล-sound with friends and family members.

Similar English sounds for rɔɔ ร: **red, reason, read**
Rating: Not very good

Different ways to transliterate rɔɔ ร
Royal Thai: r
Other transliterations: r, and often l

Summary
Initial sound: rɔɔ ร
End sound: n น
Consonant class: Low
Manner of articulation: Unaspirated, voiced, sonorant trill consonant sound
Place of articulation: Teeth (Alveolar)

Note The end sound n น is the same for the three sonorant initial sounds n น, r ร and l ล.

lɔɔ ล
Thai name: ling ลิง monkey
Consonant class: Low
End sound: n น
Key: Unaspirated, voiced, sonorant **lateral/teeth** sound

Improve
This sound is made as in the English word **left**. If you use the English way, you are quite close.

Description
Lateral sound means that the air is allowed to flow over the sides of the tongue rather than over the middle of the tongue. The blade of the tongue is placed flat behind the upper teeth against the alveolar ridge.

> **Note** Many Thai people like this sound, since it is quite easy to pronounce, and they often replace the ร-sound with the ล-sound. This can make it a bit difficult to understand which word is being used in cases where there is a similar sound with a different meaning. Often the only way to figure out the meaning is to do so from the context.

Similar English sounds for ลอ ล: **left**, **bell**, **like**
Rating: Good

Different ways to transliterate ลอ ล
Royal Thai: l
Other transliterations: l is used by most of the systems

Summary
Initial sound: ลอ ล
End sound: น น
Consonant class: Low
Manner of articulation: Unaspirated, voiced, sonorant lateral consonant sound
Place of articulation: Teeth (Alveolar)

> **Note** The end sound น น is the same for the three sonorant initial sounds น น, ร ร and ล ล.

2. Vowels

Special vowels ai ไอ and ai ใอ

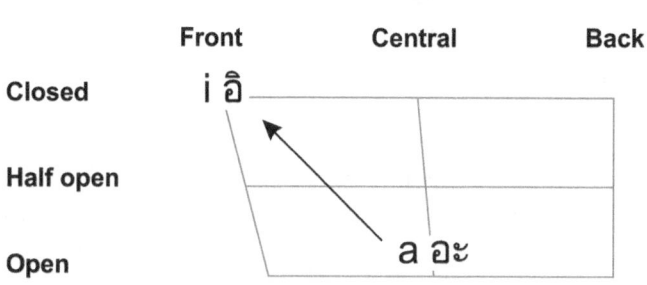

Improve
Learn to separate the short **ai** ไอ, ใอ-sound from the similar long sound **aai** อาย.

The long sound is given here just for comparison, and it is not listed in the Thai vowel list.

This sound **ai** ไอ, ใอ is made as in the English word my. If you use the English way, you are quite close.

Description
This vowel combination consists of two sounds, **à** อะ and **ì** อิ. It starts with the open unrounded vowel **à** อะ and ends with the closed **ì** อิ vowel sound.

Note There are two **ai**-sounds and symbols in the Thai vowel list, ไอ and ใอ. These two vowels are pronounced the same way, but simply have different symbols. The symbols are not interchangeable. There are only 20 words spelled with **ai** ใอ, all the rest are spelled with **ai** ไอ.

In fact, there is a third way to write this sound, **ai** วัย. This spelling is not listed in the Thai vowels list. It is considered to be a vowel combination. The long vowel combination **aai** อาย is similar, but longer.

Similar English sounds aai อาย: m**ai**, w**i**se, h**igh**
Rating: Good

Different ways to transliterate ai ใอ, ไอ
Royal Thai: ai
Other transliterations: ai, ay, uy

Summary
Vowel length: Short ai ใอ, ไอ
Manner of articulation: From open unrounded **a** อะ-sound to closed unrounded **i** อิ-sound
Place of articulation: From central to front

B. Sound exercise 12

(bɛ̀ɛp fɯ̀k-hàt thîi sìp sɔ̌ɔng แบบ ฝึก หัด ที่ สิบ สอง)

r ร rɔɔ
l ล lɔɔ

ai ใอ, ไอ
aai อาย*

* Note that the long sound is given here just for comparison. See more about long vowel combinations in Secret 16.

Examples (tuua-yàang ตัว อย่าง)
rai   ไร   something
raai   ราย   item

lǎi   ไหล   flow
lǎai   หลาย   many

Repeating sounds learned so far (phûut sám พูด ซ้ำ)
hâi   ให้   to give
dâai   ได้   to be able

| mâi | ไม่ | not |
| mâai | ม่าย | widow |

| bai | ใบ | leaf |
| bàai | บ่าย | afternoon |

| sài | ใส่ | to put on, to wear |
| sǎai | สาย | to be late |

Common expressions (kham thîi ʧái bɔ̀i-bɔ̀i คำ ที่ ใช้ บ่อยๆ)

mâi mii weelaa	ไม่ มี เวลา	I do not have time.
rɔɔ sàk-khrûu	รอ สัก ครู่	Wait a little!
pɛ́p-nɯ̀ng	แป๊บ นึง	Just a moment!
ìik sàk-khrûu	อีก สัก ครู่	In a little while.

C. Practical learning tips

Thai vowels cannot stand alone. They always need to be attached to a consonant. The consonant symbol อ is often used to show the place of a vowel in the Thai writing system. Each long Thai vowel has a short counterpart. The only difference is in the length of the sound.

When attempting to speak Thai, take it easy and don't get upset if Thai people do not understand you straight away. Particularly in tourist areas, Thais often like to practice their English instead of attempting to speak Thai. Some Thai people need you to speak almost 100 % correctly before they can understand you. Others may understand you quite easily even if you are far from perfect.

In Thai, there are a vast number of words, which sound very similar, but the meanings are totally different. Persevere! Learn to articulate clearly and you will get it right.

Politeness is an essential part of Thai culture and language. This is something westerners need to appreciate in order to be able to communicate fluently with Thai people. Be polite in every situation with everybody at all times. It is not easy to overdo. Politeness is a built-in feature of Thai language and culture. Context is also very important, you need to be aware to whom you are speaking and where.

D. Reading exercise 12

Answers from the reading exercise 11 page 138

nâu	เน่า	rotten
mɛ̂ɛn	แม่น	exact
kàu	เก่า	old
tàm	ต่ำ	low
phàu	เผ่า	tribe, clan, origin

Consonant class: Low, middle and high
End sound: Open
Vowel length: Short and long
Tone mark: máai èek ไม้เอก
Tone: Low and falling
Here we have the tone mark ' **máai èek** ไม้เอก

This tone mark is used to change the tone of **low** class consonants to the **falling** tone and the tone of **middle** or **high** class consonants to the **low** tone.

Tone rules for máai èek ไม้เอก, with low class consonant
When the word starts with a **low** class consonant, and when the tone mark is ' **máai èek** ไม้เอก, the tone is **falling**.

nâu เน่า
The word starts with the **low** class nasal sonorant consonant **n** น as in the English word **n**ote. The short special vowel **au** เอา as in the

English word n**ow**, is written so that the low class consonant n น comes between เ and า.

Tone
The tone is **falling**, since the tone mark is ` ่ ` máai èek ไม้เอก, and the word starts with a **low** consonant and ends with an **open** final sound.

Without the tone mark, the tone would be **normal**.

> **Note** All special vowels, **am** อำ, **au** เอา, **ai** ใอ,ไอ, constitute an **open** ending.

mɛ̂ɛn แม่น
The word starts with the **low** class nasal sonorant consonant m ม as in the English word **m**ake. The long vowel ɛɛ แอ-sound as in the English word s**a**d is written before the low class consonant m ม. However, the sound comes after it. The word ends with the nasal sonorant consonant n น, which constitutes an **open** final sound.

Tone
The tone is **falling**, since the word starts with a **low** class consonant, and the tone mark is ` ่ ` máai èek ไม้เอก.

Without the tone mark, the tone would be **normal**.

> **Note** All sonorant sounds, n น, m ม, ng ง, y ย, w ว, r ร and l ล, constitute an **open** final sound.

Tone rules for máai èek ไม้เอก
with middle and high class consonants
When a word or syllable starts with a **middle** or **high** class consonant, the tone mark is ` ่ ` máai èek ไม้เอก and the final sound is **open** then the tone is **low**.

kàu เก่า

The word starts with the unaspirated **middle** class consonant **k** ก as in the English word s**k**ate. The short special vowel **au** เา as in the English word n**ow** is written so that the **middle** class consonant **k** ก comes between เ and า. The special vowel **au** เา constitutes an **open** final sound.

Tone

The tone is **low**, since the word starts with a **middle** class consonant, the tone mark is ˙ **máai èek** ไม้เอก, and the final sound is **open**.

Without the tone mark, the tone would be **normal**.

Note Tone marks are usually used with an open final sound only. Note also that the consonant **k** ก is pronounced unaspirated. There is no puff of air when the sound is produced.

tàm ต่ำ low

The word starts with the unaspirated **middle** class consonant **t** ต as in the English word s**t**op. The short special vowel **am** ำ as in the English word s**um** is written after the middle class consonant **t** ต. The special vowel **am** ำ constitutes an **open** final sound.

Tone

The tone is **low**, since the word starts with a **middle** class consonant, and the tone mark is ˙ **máai èek** ไม้เอก.

Without the tone mark, the tone would be **normal**.

Note This special vowel **am** ำ is ending with the sonorant consonant **m** ม. Note also that the consonant **t** ต is pronounced unaspirated. There is no puff of air when the sound is produced.

phàu เผ่า

The word starts with the aspirated **high** class consonant **ph** ผ as in the English word **P**eter. The short special vowel **au** เา as in the English word n**ow** is written so that the high class consonant **ph**

ผ comes between เ and า. The special vowel **au** เอา constitutes an **open** final sound.

Tone

The tone is **low**, since the word starts with a **high** class consonant, and the tone mark is ˈ **máai èek** ไม้เอก.

Without the tone mark, the tone would be **rising**.

Note Tone marks are mainly used when the end sound is **open**. The same tone mark constitutes a different tone with a low class consonant than when used with a **middle** or **high** class consonant. That is to say, a specific tone mark does not denote a specific tone. Instead it acts to transform the existing tone to something else. Exactly what the new tone is will depend on the initial tone that is being transformed.

Reading exercise

Try to figure out how the following words are pronounced in Thai:

ไร้

แม้

แก้

สั้น

เข้า

The answers are given in the next Secret, page 155.

ல

Secret 13

*The sound **ng** ɴ appears in several combinations in the English language (ki**ng**, si**ng**ing, fi**ng**er etc.). However, it can prove quite difficult for English speaking learners to use this sound at the beginning of a word. This shows how strongly language skills are based on habits. You are simply not accustomed to produce this sound at the beginning of a word.*

The next sonorant sound is the nasal back sound **ng**ɔɔ ɴ. The end sound is also **ng** ɴ.

A. New sounds

I. Consonants

Sonorant nasal back sound **ng**ɔɔ ɴ
Phonetically, this consonant sound is called a voiced, unaspirated, velar nasal sound. We call it simply a "nasal back sound", since it is made at the back of the mouth, and the back of the tongue is touching the roof in the soft palate. The air is directed through the nose.

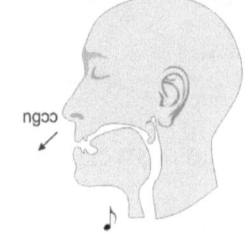

Sonorant consonant sounds ng ง

ngɔɔ ง ♪
Thai name: **nguu** ง snake
End sound: **ng** ง
Consonant class: Low
Key: Unaspirated, voiced, sonorant **nasal**/back sound

Improve

If you use the English sound as in the word si**ng**ing you are on the way. Difficulty arises from the fact that you need to learn to make this sound at the beginning of a word.

Practise saying the **m**-sound as in the English word **m**ale and note that the sound is made mainly in your nose. Your mouth is closed. Then say the **n**-sound in the English word **n**ame, and note that the tongue is touching the **front** part of your mouth. Then say the English word si**nging** and after say **nging** as you would say it normally. Now, you are already close. All you need to do is to make the sound vibrate more in your nose and let the tongue touch the **back** part of your mouth. All these sounds are **nasal sounds** meaning that the sound vibrates strongly in the nose. You may also practise this sound by saying the first part of the word si**nging** silently and the second part loudly.

Description

This consonant sound **ngɔɔ** ง is a voiced, unaspirated, velar nasal sound. It is made at the back of the mouth, and the back of the tongue is touching the roof of the soft palate. The air is directed through the nose.

Note The **ng** ง-sound does not appear at the beginning of any English words. However, in Thai it is quite common for this sound to appear at the beginning of a word.

Similar English sounds for **ngɔɔ** ง: ri**ng**ing, si**ng**ing, ki**ng**

Rating: Good, but needs some practice when at the beginning of a word

Different ways to transliterate **ngɔɔ** ง
Royal Thai: ng
Other transliterations: ng, ŋ

Summary
Intial sound: **ngɔɔ** ง
End sound: **ng** ง
Consonant class: Low
Manner of articulation: Unaspirated, voiced, sonorant nasal consonant sound
Place of articulation: Back (Velar)

Note that the end sound for **ng** ง is the same as the initial sound.

2. Diphthongs

Diphthongs ia เอียะ and iia เอีย

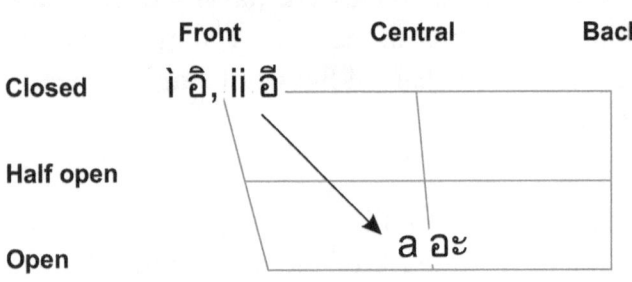

This kind of shift or glide is called a diphthong or a vowel combination.

Improve
Learn to separate the short **ia** เอียะ-sound from its long counterpart **iia** เอีย.

Short ia เอียะ-sound
Start with the pure short vowel i อิ and finish with the a อะ-sound.

Long iia เอีย-sound
Start with the pure long vowel ii อี and finish with the a อะ-sound.

Description
This sound starts from a closed, unrounded short i อิ or long ii อี-sounds and ends with the short open unrounded a อะ vowel sound. The place of articulation is from the front to the centre of the mouth.

Note that the long iia เอีย-sound is often transliterated as ia. This may be due to the fact that in rapid speech, the long ii อี-sound may not actually be that long.

Only a few words use the short ia เอียะ-sound, so there is not much chance of confusion. You may also hear something like iə or iɛ instead of iia เอีย. Standard Thai uses the iia เอีย-sound, however. Simple pure vowel sounds are never converted into anything else. When it comes to diphthongs like this, the pronunciation seems to be less precise than with pure vowel sounds.

Similar English sounds for ia เอียะ and iia เอีย: **n**ear, **h**ere, **d**eer
Rating: Not good

Different ways to transliterate
Short ia เอียะ-sound
Royal Thai: ia
Other transliterations: ia, ea

Long iia เอีย-sound
Royal Thai: ia
Other transliterations: ia, iia, ea, eea

Summary
Vowel lenght: Short ia เอียะ and long iia เอีย

Manner of articulation: From closed, unrounded short ı อิ or long ii อี-sound to short open unrounded a อะ-sound
Place of articulation: From front to centre

B. Sound exercise 13

(bὲɛp fɯ̀k-hàt thîi sìp sǎam แบบ ฝึก หัด ที่ สิบ สาม)

ng ง ngɔɔ

ia เอียะ
iia เอีย

Examples (tuua-yàang ตัว อย่าง)
ngía   เงียะ   ending particle
ngîiap   เงียบ   silent, quiet

ngía   เงียะ   ending particle
ngîiang เงียง   hook

Repeating sounds learned so far (phûut sám พูด ซ้ำ)
ngən   เงิน   money
nəən   เนิน   mound, small hill

ngong   งง   to be confused
ngóong โง้ง   to be bent

pría   เปรี๊ยะ   precisely
prîiau เปรี้ยว   sour, acid

ngai   ไง   how
ngâai   ง่าย   easy

Common expressions (kham thîi ʧái bɔ̀i-bɔ̀i คำ ที่ ใช้ บ่อยๆ)

sèt rɯ́-yang	เสร็จ รึ ยัง	Have you finished?
sèt lɛ́ɛo	เสร็จ แล้ว	Yes, I have finished.
phrɔ́ɔm lɛ́ɛo	พร้อม แล้ว	I am ready.
yang mâi sèt	ยัง ไม่ เสร็จ	No, I have not finished.

C. Practical learning tips

All high class consonants have a corresponding counterpart among the low class consonants. Therefore, the low class consonants can be divided into two groups, pair sound consonants, which have high class counterparts, and single sound consonants, which do not have any counterparts. The single sound consonants are called sonorant consonants and you need to understand this detail of classification when learning Thai.

Perhaps you will be relieved to know that Thai people themselves do not always use the correct tone when speaking in every situation. The context in which you use a particular word is very important. If you use the correct word in the right situation and pronounce it correctly, Thai people will most likely understand you even if the tone is not quite right.

Also be aware that in two-syllable words, the tone of the first syllable is often minimized and the tone of the second syllable is pronounced clearly. If you try to emphasize every tone in every syllable, your speaking will sound unnatural. See Secret 20 (22 Secrets of Learning Thai, VOL 1 – BOOK 2).

D. Reading exercise 13

Answers from the reading exercise 12 page 149

rái	ไร้	to lack, to be without
mɛ́ɛ	แม้	even, even if
kɛ̂ɛ	แก้	to untie, to fix
sân	สั้น	short
khâu	เข้า	to enter

Consonant class:	Low, middle and high
End sound:	Open
Vowel length:	Short and long
Tone mark:	máai thoo ไม้โท
Tone:	High and falling

˝ máai thoo ไม้โท

This tone mark is used to transform a **low** class consonant into the **high** tone and **middle** and **high** class consonants into the **falling** tone.

Tone rule for a low class consonant and ˝ máai thoo ไม้โท

When the word starts with a **low** class consonant, and the tone mark is ˝ máai thoo ไม้โท, the tone is **high**.

rái ไร้

The word starts with the **low** class sonorant consonant r ร as in the English word **red**. The short special vowel sound **ai** ไอ as in the English word **my** is written before the consonant r ร. However, the vowel sound comes after the consonant. The word ends with the special vowel **ai** ไอ, which constitutes an **open** final sound.

Tone

The tone is **high**, since the word starts with a **low** class consonant, and the tone mark is ˝ máai thoo ไม้โท.

Without the tone mark, the tone would be **normal**, rai ไร.

Note If you pronounce the **r ร**-sound as in the English word **red**, you are on the way. Many English speakers experience some difficulty with this sound. Please review the **r ร**-sound again. It is a rolling **r ร**, similar to the Spanish **r ร**.

mɛ́ɛ แม้
The word starts with the **low** class nasal sonorant consonant **m ม** as in the English word **man**. The long vowel sound **ɛɛ แอ** as in the English word **sad** is written before the low class consonant **m ม**. However, the sound comes after the consonant. The word ends with the long vowel sound **ɛɛ แอ**, which constitutes an **open** final sound.

Tone
The tone is **high**, since the word starts with a **low** class consonant, and the tone mark is ˇ **máai thoo ไม้โท**.

Without the tone mark, the tone would be **normal**, mɛɛ แม.

Tone rule for the middle or high class consonants and ˇ máai thoo ไม้โท
When the word starts with a **middle** or **high** class consonant, and when the tone mark is ˇ **máai thoo ไม้โท**, the tone is **falling**.

kɛ̂ɛ แก้
The word starts with the unaspirated **middle** class consonant **k ก** as in the English word **skate**. The long **ɛɛ แอ** vowel sound as in the English word **sad** is written before the consonant. However, the vowel sound comes after the consonant. The word ends with the long vowel sound **ɛɛ แอ**, which constitutes an **open** final sound.

Tone
The tone is **falling**, since the word starts with a **middle** class consonant and the tone mark is ˇ **máai thoo ไม้โท**.

Without the tone mark, the tone would be **normal**, kɛɛ แก.

> **Note** There is no puff of air when this sound is produced. Note that here the low class consonant **k** ก is not voiced as it is in the English word **go**. Try to pronounce this sound unvoiced. In Thai, there are only two voiced consonants, **b** บ and **d** ด.

sân สั้น

The word starts with the fricative **high** class consonant **s** ส as in the English word **sun**. The short vowel sound **à** อะ is written as อั above the consonant **s** ส. The word ends with the low class sonorant consonant **n** น, which constitutes an **open** final sound.

Tone

The tone is **falling** since the word starts with a **high** class consonant and the tone mark is ้ **máai thoo** ไม้โท.

Without the tone mark, the tone would be **rising**, sǎn สัน.

> **Note** Between two consonants, the short **à** อะ-sound is written as อั. Please see more about writing Thai vowel sounds in Secret 21 and about tone rules in Secret 20.

khâu เข้า

The word starts with the aspirated **high** class consonant **kh** ข as in the English word **key**. The consonant **kh** ข is pronounced strongly aspirated, and there is a clear puff of air. The special vowel sound **au** เอา as in the English word **cow** is written before and after the high class consonant **kh** ข. The word ends with the special vowel **au** เอา, which constitutes an **open** final sound.

Tone

The tone is **falling**, since the word starts with a **high** class consonant and the tone mark is ้ **máai thoo** ไม้โท.

Without the tone mark, the tone would be **rising**, khǎu เขา.

> **Note** All long vowels, special vowels and long diphthongs constitute an **open** final sound.

Reading exercise 13

Long vowels: **ii** อี, **ʉʉ** อือ, **uu** อู, **ee** เอ, **əə** เออ, **oo** โอ, **ɛɛ** แอ, **aa** อา, **ɔɔ** ออ

All special vowels: **am** อำ, **au** เอา, **ai** ใอ, ไอ

Long diphthongs: **iia** เอีย, **ʉʉa** เอือ, **uua** อัว

Reading exercise

Try to figure out how the following words are pronounced in Thai:

เป็น

เดี๋ยว

ได้

แจ๊ด

เด๋อ

The answers are given in the next Secret, page 167.

Secret 14

There are two sonorant semi-vowels in Thai, **y** ย *and* **w** ว. *At the beginning of a word or syllable, they are pronounced as consonants. However, when they appear at the end they are pronounced as vowels and form more vowel combinations.*

A complete review of all additional vowel combinations can be found in Secret 16.

The next group of sonorant sounds are the two semi-vowels **y** ย and **w** ว. The end sounds are **ù** อุ and **I** อิ respectively.

Semi vowels in the English language behave similarly as in words such as ho**w** and bo**y**.

A. New sounds

I. Semi-vowels

Sonorant semi-vowel lip sound **yɔɔ** ย
Phonetically, this consonant sound is called a voiced, unaspirated bilabial glide sound. It is produced in a similar way to the vowel **ii** อี. It glides into a vowel **I** อิ at the end of a word. It is called a semi-vowel.

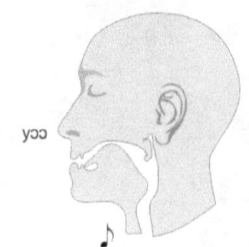

yɔɔ ย ♪
Thai name: yák ยักษ์ giant
End sound: i อิ
Consonant class: Low
Key: Unaspirated, voiced, sonorant **semi-vowel/middle** sound

Improve
This sound is made as in the English word **yes**. If you use the English way, you will be quite close.

Description
The place of articulation is palatal. The lips are kept slightly apart when this sound is produced. Glide consonants can also be regarded as vowels. There are only two glide consonants in Thai (**w** ว as in the English word **women** and **y** ย as in the English word **yes**), because they act sometimes as vowels and sometimes as consonants, they are also called semi-vowels. Each glide consonant has a vowel as a counterpart. The consonant yɔɔ ย has the vowel i อิ and the consonant wɔɔ ว has the vowel ù อุ as a counterpart.

Note We transliterate this sound with the letter **y**. Internationally and phonetically, it should be more correct to write it with the letter **j**. However, for the English speaker, it is easier to use the letter **y**, and many transliteration systems already use **y**.

Similar English sounds for yɔɔ ย: yes, hallelujah, you
Rating: Good

Different ways to transliterate yɔɔ ย
Royal Thai: y
Other transliterations: y, j

Summary
Initial sound: yɔɔ ย
End sound: i อิ

Consonant class: Low
Manner of articulation: Unaspirated, voiced, sonorant (semi-vowel), glide consonant sound
Place of articulation: Middle (Palatal)

Note that the end sound for this consonant y ย is a short vowel ไ อิ.

2. Diphthongs

Diphthongs ือa เอือะ and ืaa เอือ

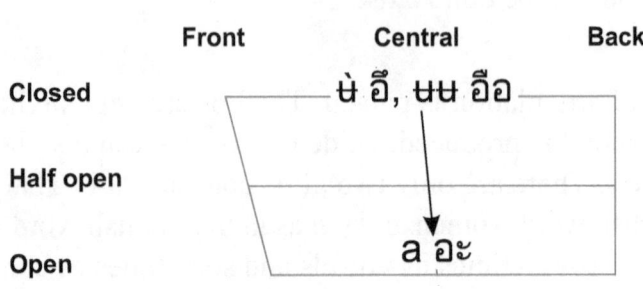

Improve

Learn to separate the short ือa เอือะ-sound from its long counterpart ืaa เอือ.

Short ือ อึ-sound
Start with the pure short vowel ือ อึ and finish with the ิa อะ-sound.

Long ืaa อือ-sound
Start with the pure long vowel ืaa อือ and finish with the ิa อะ-sound.

Go back to Secret 3 and review how to make the short ือ อึ or long ืaa อือ-sound. This sound is perhaps a bit tricky for English speakers, since it does not commonly exist in Standard British or American English. Also the short and clear ิa อะ-sound is not commonly placed at the end of a word in English. The end sound in English is usually the ิə เออะ-sound as in the word moth**er**. Sometimes even the **r**-sound is pronounced, particularly in American English.

Diphthongs ืa เ◌ือะ, ืือa เ◌ือ

You may need some pronunciation help from a native Thai teacher in order to get this sound exactly right.

Description
This sound starts from the short or long, closed, unrounded vowel sounds ื อึ or ืื อือ and ends with the short open unrounded vowel อ่ อะ-sound.

Note The long ืือa เอือ-sound is often transliterated as ืa. This may be because in rapid speech, the long ืื อือ-sound may not be that long. Only a few words use the short ืa เอือะ-sound, so there is not much possibility of confusion here.

You may often hear something like ือ or ืแ instead of ืือa เอือ. Standard Thai uses the ืือa เอือ-sound. While simple pure vowel sounds are never converted into anything else, with diphthongs, things are looser in practice.

Similar English sounds for ืa เอือะ and ืือa เอือ: **s**ure, **p**ure, **l**ure
Rating: Not good

Different ways to transliterate
Short ืa เอือะ
Royal Thai: uea
Other transliterations: ืa, uea, ืa

Long ืือa เอือ
Royal Thai: uea
Other transliterations: ืa, ื:a, ืือa, uea, ue:a, ืืa

Summary
Vowel length: Short ืa เอือะ and long ืือa เอือ diphthongs
Manner of articulation: From the short, closed, unrounded ื อึ or long unrounded ืื อือ to the short, open, unrounded อ่ อะ sound.
Place of articulation: From central to central

B. Sound exercise 14

(bɛ̀ɛp fɯ̀k-hàt thîi sìp sìi แบบ ฝึก หัด ที่ สิบ สี่)

y ย yɔɔ

ɯa เอือะ
ɯɯa เอือ

Examples (tuua-yàang ตัว อย่าง)
yɯa	เหยือะ	(only a sound, no meaning)
yɯɯa	เหยือ	victim
yɯak	เหยือก	jug, pitcher
yɯɯak	เหยือก	jug, pitcher

Note that sometimes the vowel sound of the diphthong is pronounced short, even if it is written long in Thai.

Repeating sounds learned so far (phûut sám พูด ซ้ำ)
yím	ยิ้ม	smile
yîiam	เยี่ยม	excellent
lɯ́k	ลึก	deep
lɯ̌ɯa	เหลือ	to remain
wai	ไว	fast
wǎai	หวาย	wicker palm
din	ดิน	earth
diiau	เดียว	alone

Common expressions (kham thîi ʧái bɔ̀i-bɔ̀i คำ ที่ใช้ บ่อยๆ)
thîi-nǎi	ที่ ไหน	Where?
thîi nîi	ที่ นี่	Here.
pai nǎi	ไป ไหน	Where are you going to?
pai nǎi maa	ไป ไหน มา	Where have you been?

C. Practical learning tips

The best way to learn the Thai consonant sounds is to put them into their respective groups. There are 7 middle class consonant sounds, 7 high class consonant sounds and 14 low class consonant sounds, which can be divided into 7 pair sounds and 7 single sounds.

1. First learn the seven middle consonants. These do not have any pair sound in the low consonant group. Note that they are all **unaspirated** stop sounds.

The seven middle consonants (single)
p ป, b บ, t ต, d ด, ts จ, k ก, อ*

Unaspirated consonants are made with the glottal stop. Since, for English speakers, these sounds are difficult when they occur at the beginning of words, it is advisable to learn to make these sounds with the glottal stop. See more about how to make a glottal stop on page 26.

Similar sounds in English are made aspirated at the beginning of the word.

* This symbol can function as a consonant or a vowel. When a consonant, it is a silent tone regulator and used with four words only. They are:

yàa	อย่า	do not
yùu	อยู่	to live, to stay
yàang	อย่าง	kind, sort of
yàak	อยาก	to want

2. Next, learn the seven high consonants and their low class pair sounds.

All high consonants have a pair sound in the low class consonant group. They are transliterated the same, only the tone is different. They are all **aspirated** stop or fricative sounds.

The seven high consonants (pair)
ph ผ, f ฝ, th ถ, s ส, ʧ ฉ, kh ข, h ห

The seven low consonants (pair)
ph พ, f ฟ, th ท, s ซ, ʧ ช, kh ค, h ฮ

3. Finally, learn the remaining low consonants. These are all **sonorant** sounds, meaning that the sound is not stopped or restricted, and can be prolonged indefinitely.

Seven low consonants (single, sonorant)
m ม, n น, ng ง, l ล, r ร, w ว, y ย

Learn how to have fun and you will find that the Thai language comes more easily. Thai people are generally very easygoing and polite, and you will surely be invited to join the party.

If you manage to add the following three words into your daily practice while communicating with Thai people, you are well on the way to understanding the Thai people and language.

sànùk สนุก fun
– Language and life should be "sànùk สนุก fun", otherwise Thai people do not feel very good.

sàdùuak สะดวก convenient
– Whatever is convenient and comfortable is right. There is no need to make simple things complicated.

sàbaai สบาย to feel at ease
– To feel at ease and be happy is your birth right. Note that it is perfectly normal to smile at or with strangers in Thailand, while in many western countries this is clearly not the case.

Perhaps one should add one more word.

sà-àat สะอาด to be clean and fresh
– To be and feel clean and fresh are very important personal qualities in Thailand.

D. Reading exercise 14

Answers from the reading exercise 13 page 159
Tone marks used only for the middle class consonants

pen	เป็น	to be, to be able to
dìiau	เดี่ยว	alone
dâai	ได้	can, to get, to obtain
tsɛ́ɛt	แจ๊ด	extreme, very, excessive
də̌ə	เด๋อ	clumsy, silly

Consonant class: Middle
End sound: Open or closed
Vowel length: Short and long
Tone mark: **All four tone marks**
Tone: Normal, low, falling, high and rising

We introduce two additional tone marks:
 ́máai trii ไม้ตรี and
 ̇máai tsàttàwaa ไม้จัตวา

Note that with these two additional tone marks, a middle class consonant can constitute all **five** tones. These two tone marks are used with the middle class consonant only.

The tone mark ́máai trii ไม้ตรี
This tone mark is used only with a **middle class** consonant and produces a **high tone**.

This tone mark can also be used with a **closed** final sound. All other tone marks are used when the ending is **open**.

• **máai tsàttàwaa** ไม้จัตวา
This tone mark is used only with a **middle class** consonant and produces a **rising tone**.

> *Note* These two additional tone marks can be used with a **middle class** consonant **only**. This fact is not often made very clear in Thai learning books. Sometimes these tone marks are even misused to also transform the tone of a **low** consonant. That type of spelling is incorrect.

Tone rule I for the normal tone
When a word or syllable starts with a **low** or **middle** class consonant, and when the word ends with an **open** final sound, the tone is **normal**.

pen เป็น
The word starts with the **middle** class consonant **p** ป, which is pronounced unaspirated as in the English word **spine**. The short **è** เอะ vowel sound as in the English word **pen** is written before the **middle** class consonant **p** ป. However, the vowel sound comes after the consonant. The word ends with the sonorant **low** class consonant sound **n** น, which makes an **open** final sound.

Tone
The tone is **normal**, since the word starts with a **middle** class consonant and ends with an **open** sound.

> *Note* The short **è** เอะ-sound is written with the vowel shortening symbol, which is marked above the consonant.

Tone rule for ˈ **máai èek** ไม้เอก with a middle class consonant
This tone mark turns a word or syllable starting with a **middle** class or **high** class consonants into a **low** tone and a **low** class consonants into the **falling** tone.

dìiau เดี่ยว

The word starts with the voiced **middle** class consonant **d** ด as in the English word **d**own. The long diphthong **iia** เอีย (no good English example available) is written around the **middle** class consonant **d** ด. The word ends with the **low** class sonorant semi-vowel **w** ว, which constitutes an **open** final sound.

Tone

The tone is **low**, since the word starts with a **middle** class consonant, and the tone mark is ˈ **máai èek** ไม้เอก.

Without the tone mark, the tone would be **normal**, **diiau** เดียว.

> **Note** The semi-vowel **w** ว is pronounced as **u** at the end of a word or syllable as in the English word how.

Tone rule for ˇ **máai thoo** ไม้โท with middle class consonant

This tone mark turns a word or syllable starting with a **middle** class or **high** class consonants into a **falling** tone, and a **low** class consonants into a **high** tone.

dâai ได้

The word starts with the voiced unaspirated **middle** class consonant **d** ด as in the English word **d**ate. The short special vowel **ai** ไอ as in the English word m**y** is written before the **middle** class consonant **d** ด. The vowel sound however, comes after the consonant. The word ends with the short special vowel **ai** ไอ, which makes an **open** final sound.

Tone

The tone is **falling**, since the word starts with a **middle** class consonant, and the tone mark is ˇ **máai thoo** ไม้โท.

Without the tone mark, the tone would be normal and the vowel **short**, **dai** ได.

Note The Thai spelling for the vowel sound **ai** ไอ suggests that the vowel sound **a** is short. However, the length of the vowel sound is long **aa**. The word is usually pronounced as **dâai** ได้ and not as **dâi** ได้. This is one of those irregular pronunciations in existence. There are a few words like this, and you just have to learn through usage.

All special vowels constitute an **open** final sound regardless of whether being pronounced long or short.

Tone rule for ˝ **máai trii** ไม้ตรี only with a middle class consonant
This tone mark is only used with the **middle** class consonants to transform the tone into a **high** tone.

tsɛ́ɛt แจ๊ด
The word starts with the unaspirated middle class consonant **ts** จ as in the English word **job** (not a very good example). The long **ɛɛ** แอ vowel sound as in the English word **sad** is written before the middle class consonant **ts** จ. The vowel sound **ɛɛ** แอ comes after the consonant **ts** จ, however. The word ends with the middle stop consonant **d** ด, which is transliterated as **t** ด. The final sound is **closed**, since the word ends with the stop consonant.

Tone
The tone is **high**, since the word starts with a **middle** class consonant, and the tone mark is ˝ **máai trii** ไม้ตรี.

Without the tone mark, the tone would be **low**, **tsɛ̀ɛt** แจด.

Note The end sound is the unaspirated and unvoiced stop sound **t** ด. There is no puff of air when this sound is produced.

This tone mark ˝ **máai trii** ไม้ตรี looks a bit like a vowel shortening symbol as in the word **pen** เป็น. Be careful not to mix them up.

Tone rule for ˙máai tsàttàwaa ไม้จัตวา to be used only with the middle class consonants

This tone mark is only used with the **middle** class consonants to transform the tone into a **rising** tone.

dǒə เดอ

The word starts with the voiced and unaspirated **middle** class consonant **d** ด as in the English word **d**ance. The long **əə** เออ vowel sound as in the English word h**er** (without the **r**-sound) is written before and after the **middle** class consonant **d** ด. The vowel sound **əə** เออ comes after the consonant **d** ด, however. The word ends with the long vowel sound **əə** เออ, which makes an **open** final sound.

Tone

The tone is **rising**, since the word starts with a **middle** class consonant, and the tone mark is ˙máai tsàttàwaa ไม้จัตวา.

Without the tone mark, the tone would be **normal**, **dəə** เดอ.

Note The long **əə** เออ vowel sound is also written as **dəən** เดิน (to walk) or **nəəi** เนย (butter). Please see more about how vowel sounds are written in the 21st Secret.

Reading exercise

Try to figure out how the following words are pronounced in Thai:

เร็วๆ

เบียร์

แข็ง

เสือ

เหลือ

The answers are given in the next Secret, page 177.

Secret 15

In Secrets 1–15 we review all 20 Thai consonant sounds represented by the most common 28 Thai consonants. All 7 high class consonants have a pair sound in the low class group and are transliterated the same.

However, the Thai alphabet list consists of 44 consonants. There are many imported foreign words in Thai, which are borrowed from Pali, Sanskrit, Khmer and English. These often use many different symbols to denote the same sound.

For the complete list of consonants please see Secret 22 (22 Secrets of Learning Thai, VOL 1 – BOOK 2).

A. New sounds

I. Semi-vowels

Sonorant semi-vowel lip sound wɔɔ ว
Phonetically, this consonant sound is called a voiced unaspirated bilabial glide sound. It can be also regarded as a vowel, since it is produced in a similar way to the vowel u อุ. It glides into the vowel sound u อุ at the end of a word. Because of this it is also known as a semi-vowel.

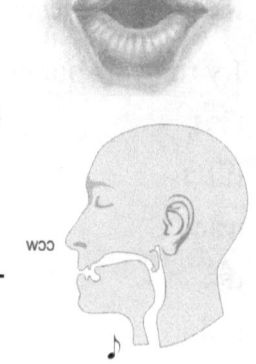

wɔɔ ว

Thai name:	wɛ̌ɛn แหวน ring
End sound:	u อุ
Consonant class:	Low
Key:	Unaspirated, voiced, sonorant **semi-vowel/lip-back** sound

Improve
This sound is made as in the English word **we**. If you use the English way, there should not be any problems.

Description
The place of articulation is bilabial, and the lips are slightly apart in the initial position. As this sound glides into the semi-vowel **wɔɔ ว**, the lips are rounded. The sound is a voiced, sonorant glide sound.

Note There are two consonants in Thai (**w ว** and **y ย**), which are also known as semi-vowels. Each semi-vowel has a corresponding vowel as its counterpart. In Thai, a **v**-sound like in the English word **v**ictory does not exist at all. Therefore, Thais would pronounce this word as **w**ictory.

Similar English sounds for wɔɔ ว: **w**oman, **w**e, q**u**een
Rating: Quite good

Different ways to transliterate wɔɔ ว
Royal Thai:	w
Other transliterations:	w is used by most of the systems.

Summary
Initial sound:	wɔɔ ว
End sound:	u อุ
Consonant class:	Low
Manner of articulation:	Unaspirated, voiced, sonorant semi-vowel glide consonant sound
Place of articulation:	Lip (Bilabial)/Back (Velar)

Note Please note that the end sound for this consonant **w** ว is a short vowel **ù** อุ.

2. Diphtongs

Diphthongs ùa อัวะ, uua อัว

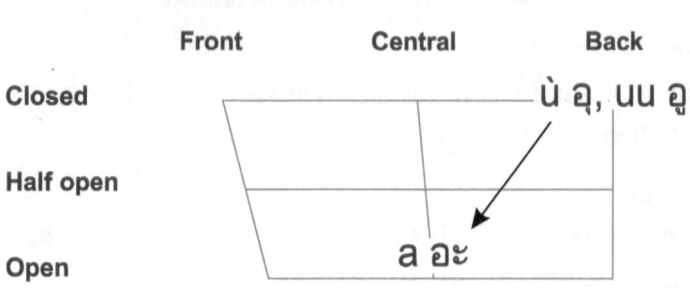

Improve
Please learn to separate the short **ùa** อัวะ-sound from its long counterpart **uua** อัว.

Short **ùa** อัวะ-sound
Start with the pure short vowel **ù** อุ and finish it with **à** อะ-sound.

Long **uua** อัว-sound
Start with the pure long vowel **uu** อู and finish it with **à** อะ-sound.

Description
This sound starts from the closed, rounded short **ù** อุ or long **uu** อู-sound, ends with the short open unrounded vowel **à** อะ-sound. The place of articulation is from the back of the mouth to the centre.

Note The long **uua** อัว-sound is often transliterated as **ua**. This maybe due to the fact that in rapid speech the long **uu** อู-sound may not be that long. There are only a few words using the short **ùa** อัวะ-sound. So, there is little possibility of confusion. You may also often hear end sounds like **uə** or **uɛ** instead of **uua** อัว. Standard Thai uses the **uua** อัว-sound. Simple pure vowel sounds are never converted to anything else. With diphthongs, things are a bit looser in practice.

Similar English sounds for ùa อัวะ and uua อัว: t**our**, p**ure**, s**ure**
Rating: Not good

Different ways to transliterate
Short ùa อัวะ
Royal Thai: ua
Other transliterations: ua, oa, ooa

Long uua อัว
Royal Thai: ua
Other transliterations: uua, ua, u:a, oa, o:a, oŏa

Summary
Vowel lenght: Short ùa อัวะ and long uua อัว
                         diphthongs
Manner of articulation: From closed rounded short ù อุ or long
                         uu อู to short open unrounded à อะ-
                         sound
Place of articulation: From back to central

B. Sound exercise 15

(bɛ̀ɛp fʉ̀k-hàt thîi sìp hâa แบบ ฝึก หัด ที่ สิบ ห้า)

wɔɔ ว

ùa อัวะ
uua อัว

Examples (tuua-yàang ตัว อย่าง)
wúa   ว้วะ   (only a sound, no meaning)
wuua   วัว   cow, bull

We need to use the ph-sound in order to give you more examples.

| phùa | ผัวะ | the sound of slapping |
| phuua | พัว | to join, to link |

The consonant **wɔɔ** ว appears in only a few words in conjunction with a diphthong.

Repeating sounds learned so far (phûut sám พูด ซ้ำ)

yúa	ยัวะ	hot tempered
yûua	ยั่ว	to provoke
kía	เกี๊ยะ	sandal with a thick sole
kiia	เกียร์	gear
nâu	เน่า	rotten
năau	หนาว	cold
ùn	อุ่น	to be warm
uuan	อวน	fishnet

Common expressions (kham thîi tʃái bɔ̀i-bɔ̀i คำ ที่ใช้ บ่อยๆ)

tsà pai thîi-năi kɔ̂ɔ-dâai
จะ ไป ที่ไหน ก็ได้   I can go anywhere.

tsà pai yùu lɛ́ɛu
จะ ไป อยู่ แล้ว   I am just going there anyway.

tsà pai yang-ngai kɔ̂ɔ-dii
จะ ไป ยังไง ก็ ดี   I will go anyhow.

tsà pai yang-ngai kɔ̂ɔ-taam
จะ ไป ยังไง ก็ ตาม   I will go there, whatever happens.

C. Practical learning tips

To learn a new language like Thai, you may need to use many methods. Learn by listening, memorising and reading. Adopt a childlike way of learning. Listen and try to figure out the meaning; ask many questions. Learn like an adult and try to understand. Learn like a teacher and start teaching yourself and perhaps also others. You need many teachers. Find your own way. There are many schools where Thai is taught to foreign learners, particularly in Bangkok. They use a variety of methods. (See the list at the end of the book.)

Don't worry if you can't remember all the tone rules at the beginning of your studies. The best way to learn them is by using them practically with words rather than simply memorising the rules in isolation from words. Just keep figuring out the right pronunciation and tone of different Thai words. If you are not sure, then check the rules. That way you will gain the necessary knowledge bit by bit in a practical way.

Do not forget to smile. The right attitude is as important as your language skills. Thai people have difficulty understanding foreigners who are too serious.

D. Reading exercise 15

Answers from the reading exercise 14 page 171

réu-réu	เร็วๆ	very fast
biia	เบียร์	beer, ale
khěng	แข็ง	hard
sǔua	เสือ	tiger
lǔua	เหลือ	to be left, to remain

Consonant class: Low, middle, high
End sound: Open
Vowel length: Short and long
Special symbols: ร์, ๆ, ร์, ห
Tone: High, normal, rising

Reading exercise 15

Here, we introduce some special symbols:

 ็ This vowel shortening symbol **máai tài khúu** ไม้ไต่คู้ is always written above the consonant, here above the consonant ร.

ๆ **máai yámók** ไม้ยมก symbol is used to repeat a word or a phrase. It is written after the word or phrase to be repeated.

 ์ This symbol is called **kaaran** การันต์ and is also written above a consonant to indicate that this written consonant is silent in speech.

ห The tone regulator **h** ห is used with the low class consonants only, and it causes the low class consonants to follow the tone rules of the high class consonants.

All these symbols are used frequently in Thai writing.

reu-reu เร็วๆ
The short vowel combination **reu** เร็ว is written with two special symbols. The symbol **máai tài khúu** ไม้ไต่คู้ is written above the consonant **r** ร. This symbol changes the long vowel sound **ee** เอ into a short vowel **è** เอะ.

The symbol, **máai yámók** ไม้ยมก is used to repeat a word or a phrase. Thais like to say **reu-reu** เร็วๆ which means very fast. There is no need to write the word twice. You simply place the symbol ๆ after the word.

Tone
The tone is **normal**, since the word starts with a **low** class consonant and ends with an **open** sound.

Note This vowel combination ends with the semi-vowel **w** ว. This is pronounced as **ù** อุ at the end of a word or syllable. All words ending with semi-vowels constitute an **open** ending.

Without these two symbols, the sound would be the long vowel combination **reeu** เรว.

biia เบียร์

The long diphthong **iia** เอีย is written around the low class consonant **b** บ. At the end of the word, there is a silent letter **r** ร์. The **r** ร-sound is made silent with the symbol called **kaaran** การันต์.

Tone

The tone is **normal**, since the word starts with a **middle** class consonant and ends with an **open** sound.

> **Note** The word **biia** เบียร์ is a loan word from English. Thais like to keep the spelling of the foreign word but change the pronunciation to better suit Thai speaking habits. Therefore, the symbol **kaaran** การันต์ is used to indicate that in this word, the letter **r** ร์ is silent in spoken Thai.

Without the **kaaran** การันต์ this word would be pronounced as **biian** เบียร. Note that the pronunciation is quite different due to the fact that the consonant **r** ร is pronounced in many different ways depending on where it stands in the word.

See more about how to pronounce the consonant **r** ร in the 21st Secret.

khɛ̌ng แข็ง

The high class consonant **kh** ข is pronounced strongly aspirated. There is a clear puff of air when the sound is produced. The long vowel sound **ɛɛ** แอ is written before the consonant **kh** ข, however, the sound comes after it. The vowel shortening symbol **máai tài khúu** ไม้ไต่คู้ is written above the consonant **kh** ข. This shortens the vowel length into the **ɛ** แอะ-sound. The word ends with the sonorant sound **ng** ง, which constitutes an **open** ending.

Tone

The tone is **rising**, since the word starts with the **high** class consonant **kh** ข, and the end sound is **open**. The vowel length does not affect the tone. The vowel sound can be either **short** or **long**.

Without the vowel shortening symbol **máai tài khúu** ไม้ไต่คู้ the word would be pronounced as **khɛ̌ɛng** แขง.

sǔua เสือ
The high class consonant **s** ส as in the English word **s**even is a fricative sound. The air is directed through a narrow channel to make a friction. The long diphthong sound **uua** เอือ (no good English examples) is written around the consonant **s** ส. However, the sound comes after it. The word ends with the long diphthong sound **uua** เอือ, which constitutes an **open** ending.

Tone
The tone is **rising** since the word starts with the **high** class consonant **s** ส, and the end sound is **open**.

Note With the **middle** and **high** class consonants the vowel sound can be either **short** or **long**, and the tone is **not** affected.

lǔua เหลือ
The sound starts with the low class consonant **l** ล as in the English word **l**ake. The long diphthong sound **uua** เอือ (no good English examples) is written around the consonant **l** ล. However, the sound comes after it. The word ends with the long diphthong sound **uua** เอือ, which constitutes an **open** ending.

Tone
The tone is **rising**, since the word starts with the **high** class consonant **h** ห, and the end sound is **open**.

There is a silent leading **high** class consonant **h** ห in front of the low consonant **l** ล. This causes the **low** class consonant **l** ล to follow the tone rules of the **high** class consonants.

Without the silent tone regulator **h** ห the tone would be **normal** **luua** เลือ, since the sound starts with a **low** class consonant, the vowel sound is **long** and the end sound **open**.

Note With the middle and high class consonants, the vowel sound can be either **short** or **long,** and the tone is **unaffected**. The tone regulator **h** ห is used with the low class consonants only.

Reading exercise

Try to figure out how the following words are pronounced in Thai:

อย่า

อยาก

หยวก

ยวบ

เงียบ

The answers are given on the next page.

Answers from the reading exercise 15 page 181

yàa	อย่า	do not
yàak	อยาก	to want
yùuak	หยวก	banana stalk
yûuap	ยวบ	to collapse
ngîiap	เงียบ	silent, quiet

Consonant class:	Low, middle and high
End sound:	Open and closed
Vowel length:	Long
Tone regulators:	**อ and ห**
Tone:	Low and falling

In the previous Secret, we already looked at the high class consonant ห, which is used as a tone regulator to change a low class consonant to follow the tone rules of a **high** class consonant.

Here, we introduce the middle class consonant อ as a tone regulator, which is used to change the tone of a **low** class consonant to follow the tone rules of a **middle** class consonant.

yàa อย่า
The sound of the word starts with the **low** class consonant **y** ย as in the English word **yes**. At the beginning of the word there is a written but silent **middle** class consonant อ, which changes the low class consonant **y** ย to follow the tone rules of a **middle** class consonant. The long vowel sound **aa** อา as in the English word **father** is written after the low class consonant **y** ย. The word ends with the long vowel **aa** อา, which constitutes an **open** final sound.

Tone
The tone is **low**, since the word starts with a silent **middle** class consonant, and when the tone mark is ' **máai èek** ไม้เอก.

Without the silent **middle** class consonant อ, the tone would be **falling**.

> **Note** The symbol อ at the beginning of the word is silent. It is a leading consonant which changes the tone rule to follow that of a middle class consonant instead of the low class consonant **y** ย. Please note that this is a rare case, since the symbol อ is normally used as vowel. When this consonant functions as a tone regulator, it is silent.

yàak อยาก

The sound of the word starts with the **low** class consonant **y** ย as in the English word yes. At the beginning of the word, there is a written but silent **middle** class consonant อ, which changes the **low** class consonant **y** ย to follow the tone rules of a **middle** class consonant. The long **aa** า vowel-sound as in the English word father is written after the low class consonant **y** ย. The word ends with the stop sound **k** ก. It is an unaspirated stop sound and constitutes a **closed** final sound.

Tone

The tone is **low**, since the word starts with a **middle** class consonant, and the word ends with a **closed** final sound.

Without the silent **middle** class consonant อ the tone would be **falling**.

> **Note** There are only four words using this feature. They are, however, used frequently and you should learn them now. They are all pronounced with a **low** tone.

yàa	อย่า	do not
yùu	อยู่	to live, to stay
yàang	อย่าง	kind, sort of
yàak	อยาก	to want

yùuak หยวก
The sound of the word starts with the **low** class consonant **y** ย-sound as in the English word yes. At the beginning of the word, there is a written but silent **high** class consonant **h** ห, which changes the low class consonant **y** ย to follow the tone rule of a **high** class consonant. The long diphthong sound **uua** อัว (no good English examples) is written after the low class consonant **y** ย, and the diphthong sound **uua** อัว comes after the consonant **y** ย. The word ends with the stop sound **k** ก, which is an unaspirated stop sound and constitutes a **closed** final sound.

Tone
The tone is **low**, since the word starts with a **high** class consonant, and the end sound is closed.

Without the silent **high** class consonant **h** ห the tone would be **falling**.

<u>Note</u> When this **high class** consonant **h** ห is written in front of a **low class** consonant at the beginning of a word, it converts the **low** class consonant to follow the tone of a **high class** consonant. There are many words which have this feature. When this consonant functions as a tone regulator, it is silent. This tone regulator is used with **low** class sonorant consonants only.

Also, with middle and high class consonants, the vowel sound can be either **short** or **long**, and the tone is **not** affected. Note that the spelling of the long diphthong **uua** อัว changes when the word ends with a consonant. The symbol อั is dropped.

yûuap ยวบ to collapse
The word starts with the **low** class consonant **y** ย as in the English word yes. The long diphthong sound **uua** อัว (no good English examples) is written after the consonant **y** ย, and the sound **uua** อัว also comes after the consonant **y** ย. The word ends with the stop

sound **b** บ, which we transliterate as **p** ป. **p** ป is an unaspirated stop sound and constitutes a **closed** final sound.

Tone
The tone is **falling**, since the word starts with a **low** class consonant, the vowel sound is **long** and the end sound is **closed**.

Note The spelling of the long diphthong **uua** อัว changes when the word ends with a consonant. The symbol อั is dropped.

ngîiap เงียบ silent, quiet
The word starts with the **low** class consonant **ng** ง as in the English word ki**ng**. The long diphthong sound **iia** เอีย (no good English examples) is written all around the consonant **ng** ง. However, the long diphthong sound **iia** เอีย comes after the consonant **ng** ง. The word ends with the stop sound **b** บ, which we transliterate as **p** ป. **p** ป is an unaspirated stop sound and constitutes a **closed** final sound.

Tone
The tone is **falling**, since the word starts with a **low** class consonant, the vowel sound is **long**, and the end sound is **closed**.

Note In English, this consonant **ng** ง does not appear at the beginning of words. You need some practice to get it right at the beginning of a word. This sound is, however, frequently used in many English words, such as si**ng**ing, taki**ng**, lo**ng**, wro**ng** etc.

Bibliography

Becker, Benjawan Poomsan. Thai for Beginners. Paiboon Publishing, California, 1995.

Becker, Benjawan Poomsan. Thai for Intermediate Learners. Paiboon Publishing, California, 1998.

Becker, Benjawan Poomsan. Thai for Advanced Learners. Paiboon Publishing, California, 2000.

Burusphat Somsonge. Reading and Writing Thai. Institute of Language and Culture for Rural Development, Mahidol University, Bangkok, 2006.

Dhyan, Manik. 22 Secrets of Learning Thai – Complete Guide to Sounds, Tones and Thai Writing System, Dolphin Books, 2014.

Dhyan, Manik. Learning Thai with hâi ให้ Dolphin Books, 2016.

Higbie, James & Thinsan Snea. Thai Reference Grammar: The Structure of Spoken Thai. Orchid Press, Bangkok, 2003.

James, Helen. Thai Reference Grammar. D.K. Editions & Suk's Editions, Bangkok, 2001.

Kanchanawan, Nitaya & Eynon, Matthew J. Learning Thai (A Unique and Practical Approach). Odeon Store, Bangkok, 2005.

Ponmanee, Sriwilai. Speaking Thai for Advanced Learner. Thai Studies Center. Chiang Mai Universtity, Chiang Mai, 2001.

Smyth, David. Thai: An Essential Grammar. Routledge, London and New York, 2002.

Smyth, David. Teach Yourself Thai. Hodder Headline, London, 2003.

22 Secrets of Learning Thai

– Complete Guide to Sounds, Tones and Thai Writing System

ISBN 978-9525572858, 359 pages

Twenty-two Secrets of Learning Thai teaches you all the sounds used in spoken and written Thai. It includes 20 consonant sounds, 18 pure vowel sounds, all special vowels and vowel combinations. It points out the main obstacles for learners, for example which Thai sounds are most difficult for an English speaker to produce. It then gives you handy tips to help overcome these difficulties. Much care has been taken to describe each sound in phonetic as well as in practical terms so that everyone should be able to grasp the correct way to produce Thai sounds.

The book has been designed so that it can be used by all levels of Thai learners. It contains a special exercise section, which teaches you in a step by step manner how to learn to read Thai script. At the same time all the Thai tone rules are taught in theory and practice. The student will get to know the most common Thai consonant symbols as well as rare symbols mostly borrowed from Indic languages, Pali and Sanskrit.

This book is also available in two seperates books as follows:

Sounds of the Thai Language Book I – Basic Sounds
(Secrets 1–15 ISBN 978-9526651323, 182 pages)

Sounds of the Thai Language Book II – Advanced Sounds
(Secrets 16–22 ISBN 978-9526651330, 178 pages)

22 Secrets of Learning Thai

– *Learning Thai with hâi ให้*

ISBN 978-9526651156, 296 pages

hâi ให้, along with words like dâai ได้, lέεu แล้ว and kɔ̂ɔ ก็, is one of the most important words in the Thai language.

When speaking Thai, it is important to understand the correct usage of the verb hâi ให้ in everyday speech.

One simple way to use the verb hâi ให้ is *to give something to someone*. It is used in a similar manner as the English verb *to give*.

In addition, hâi ให้ is used as a causative verb which has several different meanings depending on the situation, and the way it is spoken. It can be translated into English as *to let, to allow, to make* and even *to order* or *to force someone to do something*.

In some situations hâi ให้ is better translated into English as the preposition *for*, as in *for you, for me*, etc. It is also often used in idiomatic phrases where it carries no meaning itself but denotes only the sense of a command.

Thais use the verb hâi ให้ in an intuitive way in a variety of situations in order to express feelings, wishes, commands and nuances of meaning while communicating with each other every day.

If you learn this word well, you will be rewarded.

22 Secrets of Learning Thai

– *Learning Thai with dâai* ได้

Book I, Secrets 1–14

ISBN 978-9526651200 , 283 pages

Whether you are a beginner or an advanced learner, you certainly want to learn to speak Thai fluently. This book will take you a long way towards your goal.

dâai ได้ is one of the most common words in Thai. It is a multifunctional helping verb and is used by Thais in several different ways. It has many distinct meanings depending on where it is placed in a sentence and which other words are used with it. With this book you won't just learn how to use dâai ได้ but will also acquire a deeper knowledge of the Thai language in general.

Included are:
- complete and informative written examples
- audio spoken by native speakers
- highlights and explanations of dâai's ได้ usage
- sections of simple and easy to understand advice
- useful hints and tips on dâai ได้ and the spoken Thai language

Furthermore, you will get to see the language "through the eyes of dâai ได้". Study this book and you will be rewarded; your Thai friends will be amazed at your deep understanding of the subtleties of their language.

22 Secrets of Learning Thai

– *Learning Thai Tenses with dâai* ได้

Book II, Secrets 15–22

ISBN 978-9526651408 , 278 pages

Whether you are a beginner or an advanced learner, you will surely want to learn to speak Thai fluently. In order to do this, it is vital to use time words and tense markers correctly.

The English term *tense* is also a handy way to talk about past, present and future activities in Thai, even though there are no *tenses* as such in the Thai language. When compared to English, Thai tenses are expressed very differently.

It is often said that dâai ได้ denotes a past tense. However, it would be better not to think of dâai ได้ as the past tense marker since it can also be used to refer to present or future events.

To help you speak Thai fluently the Book II includes:
- complete and informative written examples
- audio spoken by native speakers
- highlights and explanations of dâai's ได้ usage
- sections of simple and easy to understand advice
- useful hints and tips on dâai ได้ and the spoken Thai language

Books I and II complement each other. However, each book has a different focus. In Book I, Secrets 1–14, we introduced dâai ได้ and explained where it should be placed in sentences. dâai ได้ has several grammatical functions; hence, it also has several meanings depending on the context. In Book II, Secrets 15–22, we focus on tenses.

Have fun while you study them both; then, you will understand how Thais express themselves in everyday life!

Learning Thai Quickly and Easily

with Original Thai Words

ISBN 978-9526651439, 320 pages

Do you want to learn to speak Thai as naturally as Thais do? Thai is not as difficult as you may think! If you follow the guidelines of this book, you will acquire a basic knowledge of the language in just a few weeks.

Students, usually, face several obstacles when studying Thai. In this book, we shall explain clearly what these obstacles are and how to overcome them. We shall also point out what you need to know and what you may ignore when learning to speak Thai. This will ensure your time and effort is focused on the things that really matter. You will be in a position to make an informed decision on how to proceed and deepen your language skills.

We use a simple and direct method which is easy to comprehend. You don't have to master the complex Thai writing system in order to speak Thai fluently. In this book, we concentrate on "original Thai words" which form a very important part of the Thai vocabulary and are used by Thais every day in conversation.

The book is designed in such a way that it can be used by both beginners and by those who have already reached intermediate level.

Included are:

• written examples and sentences • audio spoken by native speakers • highlights, explanations and examples on "how the language works" • simple and easy to understand advice • hints and tips on spoken Thai language • "Take it further" section which includes many more tips on how to proceed with your studies

Now, you can tell all your friends that learning Thai can be easy. Read this book and you will discover how!

Learning Thai Quickly and Easily

Understanding Thai Language and Grammar – Take It Further

ISBN 978-9526651460, 264 pages

Undertanding the structure and grammar of the Thai languge is very important since it may differ considerably from your own language

Included are:
- Original Thai words compared to foreign origin words
- Personal pronouns and family members
- Days, weeks, months, seasons and numbers
- Telling time – 24-hour clock compared to the Thai style
- Foods, drinks and spices
- Travelling, places, buildings and countries of the world
- Names of animals and insects
- Health words and personal items
- Adjectives, adverbs and verbs
- Thai question words, prepositions and conjunction words
- Classifiers and prefixes
- tsai ใจ heart -word
- Summary of the Thai tenses
- Words of wisdom

This book has been designed to be used as a compliment to the book "Learning Thai with Original Thai Words". It can be used, however, with any other Thai learning book.

Coming books:

22 Secrets of Learning Thai:
– Learning Thai Tenses with lέεu แล้ว
  (coming 2021 ISBN 978-9526651446)
– Learning Thai with kɔ̂ɔ ก็
  (coming 2022 ISBN 978-9526651453)

Learning Thai Quickly and Easily:
– Learning Thai with English Words
  (coming 2021 ISBN 978-9526651347)
– Learning Thai with Foreign Words
  Pali, Sanskrit, Khmer, Chinese...
  (coming 2022 ISBN 978-9526651477)

Audio spoken in MP3 format by native speakers can be downloaded from the following address: www.thaibooks.net

Thai voices: Ms. Waree Singhanart
                 Mr. Watit Pumyoo
English voice: Mr. Mark Harris

For more information

Publisher:

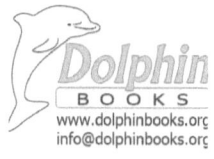

www.dolphinbooks.org
info@dolphinbooks.org

www.thaibooks.net
www.facebook.com/22Secrets

www.ingramcontent.com/pod-product-compliance
Lightning Source LLC
LaVergne TN
LVHW041939070526
838199LV00051BA/2847